No Meat, No Dairy, No Gluten

Just Flavour...
...and Goodness

No Meat, No Dairy, No Gluten
Just Flavour...
...and Goodness

WENDY HORNE

SPRING HILL

Published by Spring Hill, an imprint of How To Books Ltd
Spring Hill House, Spring Hill Road
Begbroke, Oxford OX5 1RX
United Kingdom
Tel: (01865) 375794
Fax: (01865) 379162
info@howtobooks.co.uk
www.howtobooks.co.uk

First published 2011

How To Books greatly reduce the carbon footprint of their books by sourcing their typesetting and printing in the UK.

Illustrations by Firecatcher

British Library Cataloguing in Publication Data
A catalogue record for this book is available from the British Library

ISBN: 978 1 905862 72 6

Produced for How To Books by Deer Park Productions, Tavistock, Devon
Typeset by PDQ Typesetting Ltd, Newcastle-under-Lyme, Staffordshire
Printed and bound in Great Britain by Bell & Bain Ltd, Glasgow

Contents

Introduction

Gluten and dairy intolerances are becoming more and more common as a result of our diets and lifestyles changing so much in recent years.

Gluten is a special type of protein found in rye, wheat and barley and therefore in most types of cereals and bread, which are a staple part of our British diet. A bad reaction to gluten can cause coeliac disease, an inflammation of the intestine that can be diagnosed by your doctor. However, a more general intolerance or allergic reaction can also occur. The symptoms may include bloating, migraine, fatigue, itchy skin, irritable bowel syndrome (IBS) or a variety of other unpleasant effects. Gluten intolerance can be diagnosed by a food intolerance test.

Dairy food is also a large part of our diet. Milk contains a sugar called lactose which some people are unable to digest. This causes abdominal bloating, cramps and diarrhoea or nausea. A general intolerance to milk can give a variety of symptoms such as those experienced by people who are wheat intolerant. Once again, a doctor will diagnose a lactose intolerance and a food intolerance test would show up a milk intolerance.

We eat so much processed food these days, and as a result we can be unaware of exactly what these foods actually contain. So it is important to read the labels! For example, mayonnaise does not usually contain dairy or wheat, but 'light' mayonnaise contains a wheat product to give it stability. Potato crisps in their simplest form are fine to eat but flavoured crisps often have a whey addition and are therefore unsuitable for a dairy-free person.

My answer to this minefield is to cook and eat your own food so that you know what you are putting into your body and can avoid anything to which you are intolerant. Take your own food to work instead of buying from a fast food outlet. It is much cheaper and you can make enough food at one time to eat over a few days.

It may seem problematic to cook for an exclusion diet when the rest of your family eats 'normally' but lots of the recipes in this book are for dishes that can also be served with meat, for example, and they are so tasty that they can be enjoyed by everybody. Just serve yourself a bigger helping!

If your body reacts badly to dairy or gluten products or if you have an aversion to eating meat, your pleasure in eating need not be compromised. These recipes are all about flavour and goodness and taste and, above all, enjoyment! And just because you have to eliminate dairy and gluten, your meals need not be cranky or stodgy or boring. Instead, they can be packed full of goodness and contrast, easily digested, and leave you feeling not at all deprived.

For those who have been to complementary therapy classes to nurture the mind, you will know that this way of eating does not block your inner senses, and will nurture your body too. Satvik and yoga therapists recommend this style of eating because it does not overload the body's cleansing systems, thus leaving it more open to healing.

This book includes recipes from all over the world, including India, Spain, Italy and Greece, so there is a great variety of types of food for you to enjoy. All of the recipes have been tried and tested many times by the students at the Vale Therapy Centre in Somerset and have been thoroughly approved. I hope that you will enjoy cooking and eating them.

To Penny and Michael – with luv.

Conversion Charts

Oven Temperatures			
°C	**Gas mark**	**°F**	**Temperature**
130	½	250	Very cool
140	1	275	Very cool
150	2	300	Cool
160/170	3	325	Warm
180	4	350	Moderate
190	5	375	Fairly hot
200	6	400	Fairly hot
210/220	7	425	Hot
230	8	450	Very hot
240	9	475	Very hot

Weight	
Metric (approx.)	**Imperial**
25–30g	1oz
50–55g	2oz
85g	3oz
115g	4oz
140g	5oz
175g	6oz
200g	7oz
225g	8oz
250g	9oz
280g	10oz
350g	12oz
400g	14oz
450g	16oz/1lb
1kg	2lb 4oz

Liquid Measure	
Metric (approx.)	**Imperial**
25–30ml	1 fl oz
50ml	2 fl oz
75ml	3 fl oz
100–125ml	4 fl oz
150ml	5 fl oz
175ml	6 fl oz
200ml	7 fl oz
225ml	8 fl oz
250ml	9 fl oz
300ml	10 fl oz (½ pint)
600ml	20 fl oz (1 pint)
1 litre	1¾ pints

CHAPTER 1

A Selection of Soups

For delicious creamy soups I use a product called Pure in place of butter or margarine. This can be found in most supermarkets. I also find that Marigold vegan stock powder is excellent both for flavour and because it does not include dairy or wheat and has a low salt content. A lot of the soups also contain soya milk so it is vital that you do not boil them as they will separate and not taste as nice as they should. It is best to add the soya milk at the end of making the soup, then bringing it gently up to heat again. Many of these soups are good any time of the year and others make good use of seasonal produce.

SERVES 4

Autumn Minestrone Soup

2 tablespoons olive oil
1 celery heart, sliced
1 fennel bulb, chopped
200g celeriac, peeled and diced into 1cm pieces
2 leeks, trimmed and diced
2 cloves garlic, finely chopped
3 rosemary stalks, very finely chopped or put whole into a muslin bag
400g tin borlotti beans
200g fine green beans, chopped into 1cm pieces
800ml vegetable stock
Seasoning
250g spinach (small leaves)

This soup is a complete meal when served with some fresh bread. Ideal when you feel like eating something a little more robust after the summer of salads.

1. Heat the oil in large pan. Add the celery, fennel, celeriac and leeks, and fry for 6–8 minutes until soft.
2. Add the garlic and rosemary, if chopped. Drain and rinse the borlotti beans and stir into the pan along with the green beans.
3. Add the stock, rosemary if it is in a muslin bag, season and simmer for 5 minutes. Stir in the spinach and simmer for another 5 minutes. If you are able to eat cheese, sprinkle over some grated parmesan before serving.

Butternut Squash Soup

SERVES 6

25g Pure
1 teaspoon cumin seeds (if liked)
Pinch of nutmeg
1 large butternut squash, peeled, seeded and chopped
1 white onion, chopped
1 leek, chopped
550ml vegetable stock
300ml soya milk
Sprinkle of parsley, chopped

1. Put the Pure into a saucepan and fry the cumin seeds until they pop. Add the nutmeg.
2. Then add all the vegetables and gently cook for 10 minutes.
3. Add the stock and simmer for another 10 minutes. Whizz in a liquidiser and return to the pan.
4. Stir in the soya milk and reheat without boiling. Add some chopped parsley before serving.

SERVES 4–6

Carrot and Red Pepper Soup

60g Pure
1 teaspoon curry powder
335g carrots, peeled and chopped
1 or 2 red peppers (if liked), cut in half, deseeded and roughly chopped
1 leek, chopped
1 white onion, peeled and chopped
600ml vegetable stock
150ml soya milk
1 tablespoon fresh parsley, chopped

I love this full-bodied soup with its addition of red peppers to give it that extra bit of zing! However, if you are not keen on red peppers or indeed if red peppers are not keen on you, then just use a few extra carrots.

1. Melt the Pure in a saucepan and add the curry powder. Cook for 1 minute and then add all of the vegetables.
2. Cook for 10 minutes over a low heat and then add the stock. Simmer with the pan lid on until the vegetables are soft.
3. Whizz in the liquidiser. Return to the pan, stir in the soya milk and fold the parsley through the soup. Do not boil or it will separate and spoil.

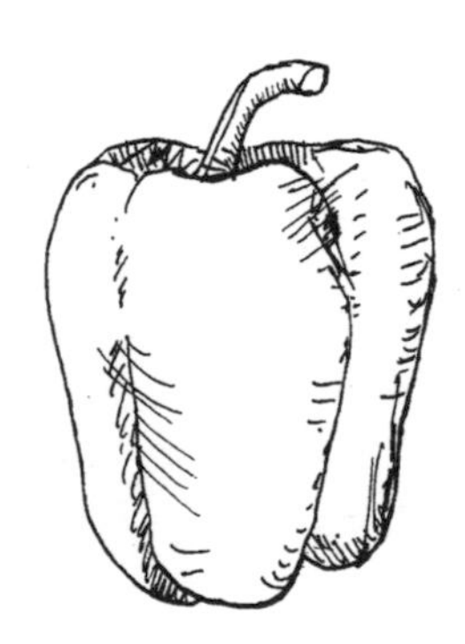

Chunky Vegetable Soup

A fantastic soup for a cold winter's day. Served in a bowl with herby dumplings, it will keep you going all day!

SERVES 4

- 30 grams of Pure
- 455g carrots, cut into 1–2cm pieces
- 1 medium onion, roughly chopped
- 1 medium swede, cut into 1–2cm pieces
- 1 small leek, cut into 1cm rounds
- ½ head of celery, chopped
- 500ml vegetable stock
- ½ bay leaf
- Good handful of mixed fresh herbs
- Good dollop of tomato purée
- 55g green or red lentils
- 30g gluten-free plain flour (optional)
- Seasoning

MAKES 16 DUMPLINGS

- 100g gluten-free self-raising flour
- 50g vegetarian suet
- 25g onion, grated
- 2 heaped teaspoons mixed dried herbs
- Seasoning

1. Melt the Pure in a saucepan and add all the vegetables. Stir well and cook for 5 minutes.
2. Add the stock, herbs, tomato purée and the lentils. Simmer gently until the vegetables are tender and the lentils are cooked.
3. If you would like the soup to be thicker, blend the flour with a little water and whisk into the hot soup. If you are adding herby dumplings then they will thicken the soup. Season well with salt and ground black pepper.
4. To make the dumplings, combine the ingredients with some salt and pepper and enough cold water to make a soft dough.
5. With floured hands, form the dough into 16 little balls. Drop them into the simmering soup and cook for about 15–20 minutes. Easy!

SERVES 4

Courgette and Carrot Soup

225g ripe tomatoes
1 tablespoon olive oil
1 tablespoon Pure
1 small white onion, chopped
3 medium carrots, peeled and grated
3 medium courgettes, finely chopped
900ml vegetable stock
Generous handful of basil and parsley, chopped

This is a nice soup for the summer and is just as good served chilled as hot.

1. Pour boiling water over the tomatoes and leave for a few minutes. Then peel and chop them.
2. Heat the oils in a saucepan and add the onion. Cook gently for 5 minutes and then add the other vegetables. Cook gently for 5 minutes and then add the stock.
3. Simmer gently until the vegetables are just cooked. Sprinkle with the chopped herbs and eat. Nice!

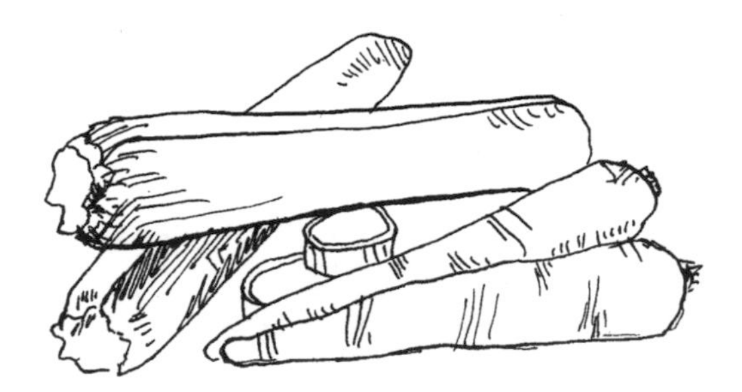

Cream of Celery Soup

SERVES 4

A lovely, clean, flavoursome soup!

30g Pure
335g celery, washed and chopped
110g potatoes, peeled and chopped
2 medium leeks, chopped
600ml vegetable stock
300ml soya milk
Seasoning

1. Melt the Pure in a saucepan and add all the vegetables. Cook gently for 10 minutes and then add the stock.
2. Simmer gently until the vegetables are soft. Whizz in the liquidiser and then return to the saucepan.
3. Stir in the soya milk, adjust the seasoning and heat gently but do not boil.

SERVES 4–6

Harira

400g tin chickpeas, drained and rinsed
1 large red onion, chopped
400g tin chopped tomatoes
140g brown lentils, soaked in water for 1 hour and then drained
½ teaspoon ground cumin
½ teaspoon turmeric
2 tablespoons harissa (not the very hot one!)
55g basmati rice
2 tablespoons gluten-free plain flour
Large pinch of saffron, soaked in 2 tablespoons lemon juice
Good handful of parsley and coriander, chopped
Extra lemon juice (optional)

A touch of the Middle East with this recipe which makes a very filling meal.

1. Put the chickpeas and chopped onion into a heavy-bottomed saucepan, cover with 1200ml water and bring to the boil.
2. Skim off any scum and then add the tomatoes, drained lentils, cumin, turmeric and harissa. Simmer until the lentils are just tender.
3. Add the rice and cook until it is just cooked.
4. Put the flour in a bowl, add 4 tablespoons of cold water and whisk together until smooth. Add the saffron lemon juice, then slowly stir this mixture into the soup and cook over a medium heat.
5. Season generously and add the herbs before serving. Add more lemon juice if desired.

Leek and Potato Soup

SERVES 4–6

A truly old English soup, which is very comforting when served in a mug to warm both hands on a cold winter's day. A slice of gluten-free bread for dipping just adds to the pleasure!

30g Pure
2 medium leeks, cleaned and chopped
1 small onion, peeled and chopped
335g potatoes, peeled and sliced
900ml vegetable stock
Pinch of mace
400ml soya milk
2 tablespoons chives, chopped

1. Melt the Pure in a saucepan and add all the vegetables. Cook gently for 10 minutes with the lid on.
2. Add the stock and mace. Simmer for 20 minutes or until the vegetables are soft. Whizz in the liquidiser until smooth.
3. Return to the saucepan, add the soya milk and reheat gently but do not boil. Add more stock if the soup is too thick for your taste. Add the chives and serve hot or well chilled.

SERVES 4

Lettuce Soup

It may sound weird to cook lettuce but, believe me, this soup tastes delicious!

55g Pure
110g white onion, chopped
335g soft variety of lettuce leaves, washed (i.e. not Iceberg)
1 tablespoon gluten-free plain flour
600ml vegetable stock
150ml soya milk
2 tablespoons chives, chopped

1. Melt the Pure in a saucepan and add the onion. Cook for 5 minutes and then add the lettuce leaves.
2. Cook gently for 10 minutes and then stir in the flour. Cook for 5 minutes and then gradually add the stock, stirring all the time, so that the flour blends in well.
3. Simmer gently for 10 minutes and then put in your liquidiser and whizz until smooth.
4. Stir in the soya milk and reheat without boiling. Garnish with chives and serve hot or chilled.

Minestrone Primavera with Pesto

SERVES 4

A delicious summer soup to make when beans are plentiful.

1. Put all of the pesto ingredients into a blender and whizz until smooth.
2. Fry the celery, onions and potatoes in the olive oil, until just tender.
3. Blanch the peas, broad beans, green beans and asparagus in salted water for a few minutes.
4. Add to the pan, cook for 5 minutes and then add the stock and the chopped mint. Simmer for 15 minutes.
5. Swirl the pesto into each bowl of soup before serving.

Pesto sauce
50g fresh basil leaves
1 large clove garlic, crushed
1 tablespoon pine kernels
6 tablespoons olive oil
Salt and pepper

Soup
½ head celery, finely chopped
2 medium onions, finely chopped
200g waxy potatoes, chopped into 1cm pieces
1–2 tablespoons olive oil
100g peas
100g broad beans
150g fine green beans, chopped into 2cm pieces
150g asparagus, chopped into 2cm pieces
500ml vegetable stock
Handful of mint, freshly chopped

SERVES 4

Moroccan Tomato and Chickpea Soup

A delicious main meal soup that is wonderfully filling and satisfying. It originated from the Eden Project in Cornwall.

1 tablespoon olive oil
1 large onion, finely chopped
1 clove garlic, finely chopped
Pinch of cayenne
Pinch of mixed spice
1 level teaspoon ground coriander
410g chickpeas, drained
850ml vegetable stock
500g passata
50g basmati rice
1 teaspoon caster sugar
1 teaspoon white wine vinegar
Seasoning

1. Put the olive oil in a saucepan, add the onion and garlic and cook gently for 10 minutes.
2. Add the spices and cook for 5 minutes.
3. Add the chickpeas, stock and passata and then simmer uncovered for 30 minutes. Add the rice and cook until tender (approximately 10 minutes). Add the sugar and vinegar and season to taste.

Mushroom Soup

SERVES 3–4

When mushrooms are cheap in the shops this is a really good-value soup. It is also very good poured over gluten-free pasta with some extra chopped mushrooms fried and added at the end of the soup's cooking time.

30g Pure
2 cloves garlic, chopped
225g dark mushrooms, chopped
30g gluten-free flour
300ml vegetable stock
300ml soya milk
1 tablespoon parsley, chopped
Seasoning

1. Melt the Pure in a saucepan. Add the chopped garlic and cook gently for 5 minutes.
2. Add the chopped mushrooms and gently cook for 10 minutes with the pan lid on.
3. Add the flour and stir well. Slowly add the stock, stirring all the time, until well blended. Bring to the boil and then simmer for 15 minutes with the lid on.
4. Whizz in the liquidiser. Return to the pan, mix in the soya milk and reheat gently. Add the chopped parsley and adjust the seasoning.

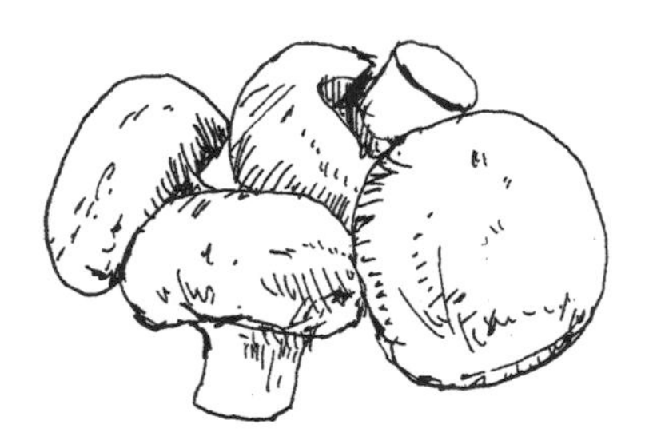

SERVES 4

620g very ripe tomatoes
Seasoning
20g basil leaves
4 tablespoons olive oil
1 teaspoon balsamic vinegar
1 fat clove garlic, finely chopped
115g potatoes, peeled and chopped
1 heaped teaspoon tomato purée
1 litre passata

Basil purée (optional)
Approx. 10g basil leaves
½–1 teaspoon salt to taste
2 tablespoons olive oil
1 tablespoon balsamic vinegar

Rich Tomato Soup

This is best made when the tomatoes are full and very ripe from all that sunshine (we hope!).

1. Turn on your oven to 220°C. Skin the tomatoes: pour over boiling water, leave them for 2 minutes and then peel off the skin. Slice the skinned tomatoes in half, put them in a roasting dish, cut-side up, with salt and pepper.
2. Dip the basil leaves in some olive oil and place on the tomatoes. Then drizzle over the rest of the oil, the balsamic and sprinkle over the garlic. Roast for about 50–60 minutes until slightly blackened (this concentrates the flavour).
3. Meanwhile, cook the potatoes in 400ml water with the tomato purée and some salt. Simmer for 20 minutes and put to one side but do not drain.
4. Whizz the potatoes, water, tomatoes and passata in a liquidiser. Season to taste, reheat and it is ready!
5. Basil purée makes a delicious accompaniment to this soup. For this, bash the basil with salt until puréed. Add the olive oil and balsamic vinegar and stir well. Gorgeously Mediterranean and summery to enjoy alfresco or al-anywhere!

Spiced Butternut Squash Soup with Coconut

SERVES 4

This is my favourite soup of all time. It has everything – easy to make, full of body, nice and spicy with a creamy taste and suitable all the year round.

25g Pure
1 medium onion, chopped
1 teaspoon curry powder
1kg butternut squash, peeled, deseeded and chopped
725ml vegetable stock
400g tin coconut milk
Seasoning

1. Melt the Pure in a large saucepan and fry the onion and the curry powder for a few minutes.
2. Add the squash and stock. Simmer gently with the saucepan lid on until the vegetables are cooked.
3. Liquidise the mixture and return it to the pan. Add the coconut milk and seasoning and reheat. Scrumptious!

SERVES 8

Spinach Soup

1kg spinach leaves
40g Pure
3 tablespoons olive oil
1200ml vegetable stock
Pinch of nutmeg, freshly grated
300ml soya milk
Salt and pepper

This soup is wonderfully velvety and I often make it when we have a glut of spinach in our allotment. If you don't have a garden, buy the cheaper variety of spinach in the shop rather than the expensive salad variety. This soup can also make a very good sauce to serve cold with vegetable terrines – just add less of the soya milk to keep the thickness.

1. Wash the spinach and drain. Melt the Pure and the olive oil, add the spinach and allow it to cook down.
2. Add the vegetable stock and cook gently with the pan lid on for about 25 minutes.
3. Add the nutmeg and whizz in the liquidiser. Return to the pan and add the soya milk. Check the seasoning and heat gently but do not boil.

Watercress Soup

SERVES 4

This is a wonderful soup to make in the watercress season. Buy bunches rather than the posh packets sold for salad. It is also delicious served chilled.

2 large bunches watercress
28g Pure
1 small onion, chopped
335g potatoes, peeled and diced
850ml vegetable stock
400ml soya milk
Seasoning

1. Cut off the coarse stalks of the cress and then chop the remainder.
2. Melt the Pure in a saucepan and gently cook the onion and watercress until soft (about 15 minutes).
3. Add the potatoes and stock and simmer with the lid on for about 30 minutes until the potatoes are soft.
4. Liquidise, return to the pan, add the soya milk and season. Reheat gently but do not boil. Simple, quick, velvety and so delicious!

CHAPTER 2

A Sprinkling of Salads

Salads are so versatile these days and bear little resemblance to the salad of yester year, which was something composed of lettuce and tomatoes and went with a slice of ham!

Some of these salads are a complete dish on their own, some are suitable for eating winter and summer, but all of them are so nutritious and can be enjoyed by everybody regardless of many food intolerances. Just try to eat seasonally to keep costs down a bit.

Apple and Celeriac Remoulade

SERVES 4

450g celeriac
3 tablespoons rapeseed oil
1 teaspoon cider vinegar
Good pinch of salt
2 sweet apples (e.g. russets)
1 tablespoon walnuts, roughly chopped
1 tablespoon parsley, chopped

This makes a very simple starter dish – it's crisp and delicious.

1. Peel the celeriac and slice as thick as a £1 coin. Then cut into matchsticks and put into a bowl of cold water.
2. In a saucepan bring ½ litre of salted water to the boil, add the celeriac and cook until just tender. Drain well.
3. Mix the oil, vinegar and salt and add to the hot celeriac. Leave to cool.
4. Quarter and slice the apples and mix with the celeriac. Arrange on a dish, or individual plates, and sprinkle over the nuts and parsley.

SERVES 6

Asparagus, Pea and Mint Rice Salad

150ml wild basmati rice
300ml salted water
2 shallots, chopped
Zest and juice of 1 lemon
3 tablespoons olive oil
Good handful of mint, freshly chopped
170g asparagus, trimmed to the spears
100g frozen peas

In the summer, this is a fantastic salad with its fresh minty and lemon flavour.

1. Cook the rice in the salted water. Drain and spread out on a tray to dry.
2. Mix together the shallots, lemon zest and juice, oil and mint. Put into a bowl with the cooled rice.
3. Boil a pan of salted water, chop the trimmed asparagus into 3cm pieces and cook for 2–3 minutes until just tender. Drain and cool.
4. Add the peas to a pan of boiling salted water and bring back to the boil. Drain and cool.
5. Add the vegetables to the rice and fold together.

Broccoli, Red Onion, Cranberry and Almond Salad

SERVES 4–6

You may not think that cold broccoli would be a good choice for a salad, but combined with the sharp cranberries, a really tasty dressing and crisp almonds it is a delight!

400g broccoli florets
1 teaspoon Dijon mustard
1 tablespoon white wine vinegar
Salt and pepper
4 tablespoons olive oil
Handful of dried cranberries
1 small red onion, finely sliced into rings
55g toasted flaked almonds

1. Mix the mustard, vinegar, salt and pepper and whisk in the oil. Marinate the cranberries in this mixture for 2 hours.
2. Blanch or steam the broccoli until only just done and then plunge into cold water and drain.
3. Then toss together the broccoli and onion rings with the marinated cranberries. Scatter over the almond flakes.

SERVES 10–12

Chickpea and Turmeric Rice Salad

2 tablespoons vegetable oil
1 small onion, chopped
1 small red pepper, chopped
1 clove garlic, finely chopped
225g basmati rice
750ml vegetable stock
2 heaped teaspoons turmeric
100g green beans, sliced into 3cm pieces
½ head of broccoli florets
410g tin chickpeas, drained and rinsed
Seasoning
Juice and zest of 1 lemon
½ good sized bunch fresh coriander, chopped

Forget about boring rice salads with the odd pea floating around! This is really colourful and tasty.

1. Heat the oil in a deep frying pan. Add the onion and fry gently until soft.
2. Add the red pepper and garlic and fry for 2 minutes. Add the rice and stir to coat. Add the stock and the turmeric and simmer for 15 minutes.
3. Blanch the beans and the broccoli in a little boiling salted water for about 5 minutes.
4. Add the chickpeas and the vegetables to the rice and continue cooking until the vegetables are tender and the rice just cooked.
5. Season and add the lemon zest and juice along with the coriander.

Chicory, Watercress, Fennel, Red Onion and Orange Salad

SERVES 4–6

Beautiful colours and fresh ingredients make this salad go with anything!

1 clove garlic
3 tablespoons olive oil
Seasoning
2–3 oranges, peeled and sliced or chopped
2 heads of chicory, sliced
1 fennel, finely chopped
1 red onion, thinly sliced into rounds
85g watercress

1. Rub the garlic around the salad bowl and then chop it and put into the bowl. Add the oil and seasoning and then the oranges.
2. Layer up the chicory, fennel and red onion in the bowl. Just before serving, toss into the orange dressing and fold in the watercress.

SERVES 6

Chinese Beansprout Salad with Soy Dressing

This salad has a really flavoursome dressing which makes it a little special.

225g fresh beansprouts
1 small red pepper, finely chopped
15cm of cucumber, unpeeled but diced
1 small red onion, thinly sliced into rings
85g fresh watercress

Dressing
½ teaspoon ground ginger
½ small onion, finely chopped
150ml olive oil
50ml red wine vinegar
2 tablespoons gluten-free Japanese soy sauce
1 small stick celery, finely chopped
2 teaspoons tomato purée
2 teaspoons lemon juice
Seasoning

1. Put the beansprouts, pepper, cucumber, onion and watercress in a serving dish. Season and then cover and chill.
2. Put all of the dressing ingredients in a liquidiser with 60ml of water and salt and pepper. Whizz and then taste and adjust the seasoning.
3. Add this dressing to the salad just before serving. Toss lightly and enjoy.

Fruity Coleslaw

SERVES 8 GENEROUSLY

I tried this recipe out on my friend's children and they loved it. It really ups the ante as far as coleslaw is concerned!

- 8 tablespoons mayonnaise
- 2 cloves garlic, finely chopped
- Juice of 1 lemon
- Drizzle of honey
- Seasoning
- 335g white cabbage, finely sliced
- 2 carrots, grated
- 1 small onion, finely chopped
- 3 sticks celery, finely chopped
- 1 sharp apple, grated
- Small handful of raisins
- 2 tablespoons pumpkin seeds
- 2 tablespoons poppy seeds
- 1 small orange, peeled and chopped

1. Put the mayonnaise, garlic, lemon juice and honey in a bowl. Whisk together and season.
2. Put the cabbage, carrots, onion, celery and apple into a large bowl. Add the raisins, seeds and the orange.
3. Pour the dressing over and mix well.

SERVES 6 GENEROUSLY

Green Bean Salad

60g green beans, cut into 3cm lengths
60g runner beans
60g peas
60g mange tout, cut into 3cm lengths
2 tablespoons olive oil
1 garlic clove, finely chopped
60g courgettes, chopped into rounds
60g tinned flageolet beans
2 tablespoons olive oil
3/4 tsp coriander seeds, crushed
½ teaspoon mustard seeds
½ small red onion, chopped
1 small mild red chilli, de-seeded and finely chopped
Zest of ½ lemon
3/4 tablespoon tarragon, chopped
Seasoning

A very tasty and spicy salad, which is perfect when you have a glut of beans and courgettes from the garden (if you are lucky enough to have one). If you have to buy the vegetables, it is still worth taking the time to make it.

1. Blanch the green and runner beans. Drain and run cold water over them, and leave to drain again.
2. Blanch the peas and mange touts. Drain and run cold water over them, and leave to drain again.
3. Fry the courgettes in 1 tablespoon of olive oil and the garlic until slightly charred.
4. Combine all the vegetables in a bowl and add the flageolet beans.
5. Put 1 tablespoon of oil in a small saucepan and add the coriander and mustard seeds. When the seeds pop, pour the flavoured oil over the vegetables.
6. Add the red onion, chilli, lemon zest and tarragon. Toss together and season.

Green Olive, Walnut and Pomegranate Salad

SERVES 8–10

This is an amazing salad with real oomph in the way of taste and texture. A lot of supermarkets now sell pomegranate seeds in packets, which is a good way to get really ripe seeds.

170g walnuts
110g pitted green olives, washed and roughly chopped
55g shelled pistachios, coarsely chopped
110g pomegranate seeds
2 small shallots, finely diced
1 red chilli, seeded and finely chopped
1 tablespoon flat parsley, finely chopped
1 tablespoon olive oil
1 tablespoon walnut oil
Splash of pomegranate molasses or ordinary molasses
Juice of 1 lemon

1. Roast the walnuts and chop coarsely.
2. Combine all the ingredients. It's that easy!

SERVES 6 GENEROUSLY

Guacamole

6 ripe avocados
1 small onion, grated
4 cloves garlic, chopped
2 tablespoons lemon juice
2 tablespoons olive oil
2 small red chillies, deseeded and chopped (or 1 if you prefer a milder taste)
Salt and freshly ground black pepper

Spread this on bruschetta, serve with a buffet, use as a dip – it is such a good all-round dish to make. Ensure that the avocados are just ripe; that they are a nice green and not too dark.

1. Core the avocados, peel and chop them and then put into your liquidiser.
2. Add all the other ingredients and liquidise to the texture you prefer. It can be rough or smooth. Chill and eat – lots!

Pasta Salad

SERVES 8–10

Pasta dishes used to be a complete no no for those who were gluten intolerant. Now, all sorts of gluten-free pastas are available in the health food shops and supermarkets, which is good news.

455g gluten-free pasta curls
2 tablespoons olive oil
Salt
225g onion, chopped
4 cloves garlic, chopped
225g mushrooms, sliced
225g courgettes, cut into rounds
400g tin chopped tomatoes
300ml passata
2 tablespoons fresh basil, chopped
French dressing
Seasoning
Parsley or basil to garnish, chopped

1. Cook the pasta in plenty of water, with 1 tablespoon of oil and salt, until just done. Then pour it into a colander, wash through in cold water and leave to drain.
2. Heat 1 tablespoon of oil in a large, thick-bottomed saucepan. Add the onion and garlic and cook for 5 minutes.
3. Add the mushrooms and cook for another 5 minutes.
4. Add the courgettes and cook for 5 minutes. Now add the tomatoes, passata and chopped basil. Bring to the boil and then simmer for 10 minutes.
5. Add the pasta, stir well and leave to cool. If you want to eat this dish hot, as a main meal, then just season and eat it now!
6. For a salad, cool and add some French dressing, just enough to add piquancy. Season and finish with a sprinkle of chopped parsley or some more chopped basil.

SERVES 6–8

Pesto Rice Salad

240ml Arborio rice
1 quantity of pesto sauce (see recipe in Chapter 7)
480ml vegetable stock
1 teaspoon salt
Juice and finely grated rind of 1 lemon
2 tablespoons olive oil
4 spring onions, finely chopped
Fresh basil leaves to garnish, torn

I could eat this whole bowl full! It is so delicious! Most commercially produced pesto sauces contain dairy products so make your own – it's very easy. (See Chapter 7 'Odds and Ends' for the recipe.)

1. Add ¼ of the pesto sauce to the dry rice and stir well.
2. Put into a deep frying pan with the vegetable stock. Stir in the salt and cover. Heat to boiling and then turn down and cook for 20 minutes with the lid on.
3. Take off the lid and put aside for 5 minutes. Pour over the remaining pesto sauce, lemon juice, rind and olive oil.
4. Sprinkle with the spring onions and basil.

Potato and Chard Salad with a Pea Pesto

SERVES 8

This is a terrific version of potato salad and is best made the day before to allow the flavours to develop.

1kg small, waxy, new potatoes
Salt and pepper
Mint
500g Swiss chard or small-leaf spinach, de-stemmed
300g frozen peas, thawed
6 tablespoons olive oil
Handful of basil
Juice and zest of 1 lemon
1 tablespoon grated ginger root
1 clove garlic, chopped
Extra lemon and basil to garnish

1. Cook the potatoes in salted and minted water. Then cool, peel and dice into large cubes.
2. Wash the chard and drain in a colander. Put into a large, thick-bottomed saucepan and cook over a gentle heat, stirring occasionally, until the chard has wilted. Drain thoroughly.
3. Put the peas in a blender with 5 tablespoons of olive oil, basil, lemon juice and zest, ginger and garlic. Season and then whizz. Put this pesto into the fridge and leave to chill and for the flavours to develop.
4. Fold the diced potatoes into the chard and then into the pesto. Put into your serving bowl and decorate with lemon slivers and some fresh basil.

SERVES 12 GENEROUSLY

Roasted Cashew Nut and Spinach Rice

100g cashew nuts
75ml olive oil
½ red onion, finely chopped
150g brown basmati rice
10g raisins
4 sticks celery, finely diced
1 orange pepper, chopped
150g cherry tomatoes, halved
200g salad spinach, roughly chopped
75ml wheat-free soya sauce
Zest and juice of 1 lemon
Seasoning
Extra lemon juice to serve

Adding freshly roasted nuts to salads really adds to the flavours and this is the case here. This salad is delicious, especially if left overnight in a cool place to allow the flavours to develop.

1. Roast the cashews and cool.
2. Cook the rice in boiling salted water. Meanwhile, put a little oil in a pan and cook the onion until soft. When the rice is ready, drain and add to the pan with the onion. Cook for 2 minutes and then add all the other ingredients.
3. Remove from the heat, season and add more lemon juice if required.

SERVES 12

Roasted Mediterranean Vegetable Salad

This is a nice winter roast vegetable salad, but in the summer it is equally as good with courgette in place of fennel and carrot instead of aubergine. In fact, any variety of chunky vegetables are really good.

3 fennel bulbs
3 aubergines
3 red peppers
3 red onions
3 garlic bulbs, peeled and chopped finely
Olive oil
Seasoning
3 tablespoons balsamic vinegar
Generous handful of basil or mint, freshly chopped

1. Preheat the oven to 225°C. Parboil the fennel and chop all the vegetables into 4cm-sized chunks.
2. Put the vegetables and the chopped garlic into a large baking tin. Toss in a generous amount of olive oil. Season well and roast for 20–30 minutes until tender, turning occasionally.
3. Remove from the oven and sprinkle with the balsamic vinegar. Toss and cool. Then sprinkle over the herbs.

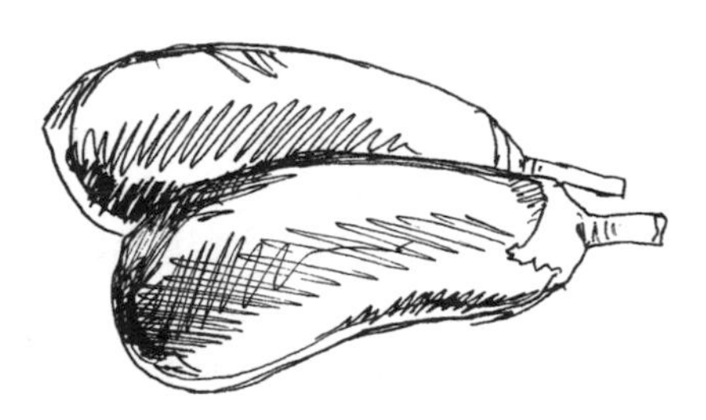

SERVES 6

Roasted Red Pepper and Lentil Salad

2 large red peppers, halved and seeded
4 tablespoons olive oil
1 tablespoon balsamic vinegar
½ small onion, finely chopped
1 stick celery, finely chopped
1 clove garlic, finely chopped
125g Puy lentils
3 sprigs of thyme
1 bay leaf
280ml vegetable stock
Squeeze of lemon juice
4 tablespoons vinaigrette
3 tablespoons parsley, chopped
2 tablespoons walnuts, roughly chopped (optional)

This glorious salad is packed full of wonderful garlicky flavour and, when sprinkled with walnuts, it is a light meal in itself.

1. Preheat your oven to 220°C. Then roast the peppers with 3 tablespoons of olive oil and a good slug of balsamic vinegar, until slightly charred. This takes about 20–30 minutes and your aim is to get a good intense flavour and for the peppers to be tender but not mushy. Cut into broad bands and leave in the juices.

2. In a saucepan, heat 1 tablespoon of oil and sauté the onion, celery and garlic until soft.

3. Add the lentils and mix in the thyme and bay leaf. Add the stock and simmer until just tender.

4. When cooked, remove from the heat, add the lemon juice, vinaigrette and the peppers and their juices. Sprinkle with chopped parsley and also walnuts, if you like. This is divine if you leave overnight to let the flavours amalgamate.

5. If you can eat dairy, cubed feta cheese can be sprinkled over the top before serving.

Roasted Tomato and Red Pepper Salad

SERVES 6

This is a real taste of Greek holidays! It is at its best towards the end of the summer when the tomatoes are full of sunshine and sweetness.

3 red peppers
500g ripe tomatoes
110ml olive oil
2 tablespoons balsamic vinegar
2 heaped teaspoons thyme, chopped
Salt and pepper
2 teaspoons soft brown sugar
1 teaspoon ground cinnamon
1 bunch parsley, chopped

1. Cut the red peppers in half and remove the seeds. Cook under a really hot grill until they are well charred and then cut into thinnish slices and leave to cool.
2. Turn the oven to 180°C. Halve the tomatoes lengthways and put into a roasting tin.
3. Whisk together the olive oil, 1 tablespoon of vinegar, thyme and salt and pepper, to taste, and pour the mixture over the tomatoes. Turn them in the oil and arrange cut-side up.
4. Sprinkle the sugar over and cook for about 45 minutes. Then leave to cool in the juices.
5. Drain the juices from the tomatoes and whisk into them another tablespoon of vinegar and 1 teaspoon of ground cinnamon.
6. Layer the tomatoes, peppers and parsley in your serving bowl, and pour over the dressing. Leave for the flavours to develop and then serve at room temperature.

SERVES 6

Spiced Chickpea Salad

1 tablespoon olive oil
1 onion, finely chopped
2 level teaspoons turmeric
1 level tablespoon cumin seeds
400g tin chickpeas, drained and rinsed
1 tablespoon lemon juice
455g fresh tomatoes, skinned and chopped
4 level tablespoons fresh coriander, chopped

Especially good served with dishes such as Curried Nut Terrine or Little Lentil Pies.

1. Sauté the onion in the oil and then add the turmeric and cumin seeds. Cook for 2 minutes and then add all the other ingredients, except for the coriander. Cook together for about 3 minutes.
2. Season and garnish with the coriander.

Spicy Red Cabbage and Apple Salad

SERVES 20

As this salad freezes well, it is worth making the whole batch. It can be reheated and served as a vegetable and is especially good at Christmas time with some chopped chestnuts sprinkled over or through.

30g Pure
1 tablespoon olive oil
1 large onion, chopped
335g cooking apple, peeled and chopped
650g red cabbage, shredded
250ml orange juice mixed with 200ml water
Pinch of ground cloves
1 teaspoon ground cinnamon
55g sultanas
1 tablespoon dark brown sugar
1 tablespoon red wine vinegar
Seasoning
Chopped walnuts and parsley to serve

1. Melt the pure and the oil in a large saucepan and add the onion. Cook for 5 minutes. Add the apple, stir and cook for 2 minutes.
2. Add the cabbage, orange juice and water, and then stir in the spices, sultanas, sugar and vinegar. Cook gently with the saucepan lid on for approx. 1 hour. Then check the seasoning and chill.
3. Garnish with chopped walnuts and chopped parsley.

SERVES 6–8

Super Salad

30g quinoa
200g broccoli florets or asparagus or a mixture of both
120g frozen peas
2 dessertspoons lemon juice
4 dessertspoons olive oil
Handful of mint, chopped
50g avocado, cut into bite-sized pieces
100g cucumber, sliced into batons
20g alfalfa sprouts or mustard cress
2 tablespoons flat leaf parsley, roughly chopped
Salt and pepper

This salad contains just about everything to keep you healthy! If you can eat goat's cheese, then chop and add to this delicious meal.

1. Simmer the quinoa in 90ml of salted water until the water has been absorbed. Fluff up with a fork and leave to cool.
2. Cook the broccoli/asparagus in 3cm of boiling water until only just cooked and still firm. Drain and rinse in cold water.
3. Cook the peas in the same way and then drain and rinse.
4. Whisk together the lemon juice, olive oil and mint and pour it into a pretty serving dish.
5. Add the avocado, followed by the cucumber and quinoa. Then put in a layer of broccoli, asparagus and peas.
6. Finally, top with the alfafa sprouts or mustard cress. At this stage you can cover the bowl with cling film and refrigerate for 2–3 hours.
7. Just before serving, season and toss the salad by using a couple of spoons to gently bring the dressing up from the bottom of the bowl. Sprinkle over the flat leaf parsley and add diced cheese if you like.

Tomato and Cucumber Salad

SERVES 4–6

This is very good as a side salad for a curry, Chickpea Patties or the Roasted Hazelnut Burgers.

½ cucumber, peeled and chopped
2 tomatoes, finely chopped
1 bunch spring onions, peeled and chopped
1 tablespoon lemon juice
1 tablespoon olive oil
¼ teaspoon salt
¼ teaspoon ground black pepper
1 tablespoon chopped coriander
30g roasted salted peanuts

1. Combine the chopped cucumber, tomatoes and spring onions.
2. Whisk together the lemon juice, olive oil, salt, pepper and coriander and pour this dressing over the salad before serving. Sprinkle with peanuts.

SERVES 4 GENEROUSLY

Warm Leek and Bean Salad

5 tablespoons rapeseed oil
2 large leeks, finely sliced
Good pinch of salt
410g tin white beans (e.g. flageolet)
1 tablespoon Dijon mustard
1 teaspoon wholegrain mustard
2 teaspoons cider vinegar
Pinch of caster sugar
2 tablespoons flat leaf parsley, chopped

A simple warm salad to make as an accompaniment to the terrines, tarts or even to meats if you are not a vegetarian.

1. Heat 2 tablespoons of the oil in a fry pan and add the leeks and salt. When the leeks begin to soften, turn down the heat and cook for 10 minutes, stirring from time to time until they are soft but not coloured.
2. Drain and rinse the beans and fold into the leek mixture. Transfer to your serving dish.
3. Whisk together the remaining ingredients and pour over the leeks. Sprinkle with parsley.

Winter Root Salad

SERVES 10

The dressing really makes this salad taste so good.

455g swede, cut into 1cm slices
455g parsnips, cut into 1cm rings
225g carrots, cut into thin strips
335g red cabbage, very thinly sliced
1 fennel bulb, thinly sliced

Dressing
30g hazelnuts, chopped
4 teaspoons red wine vinegar
4 rounded teaspoons wholegrain mustard
2 teaspoons clear honey
1 garlic head, peeled and crushed
8 tablespoons olive oil
Salt and pepper

1. Cook the swede, parsnip and carrot in salted water for just a few minutes. The vegetables must still have 'bite'. Drain and put in your serving dish.
2. Put all of the dressing ingredients in a jar and shake well. Leave to stand for about half an hour.
3. Add the raw cabbage and fennel to the root vegetables. Add two-thirds of the dressing, mix well and leave to stand for 1 hour. Add the remaining dressing.

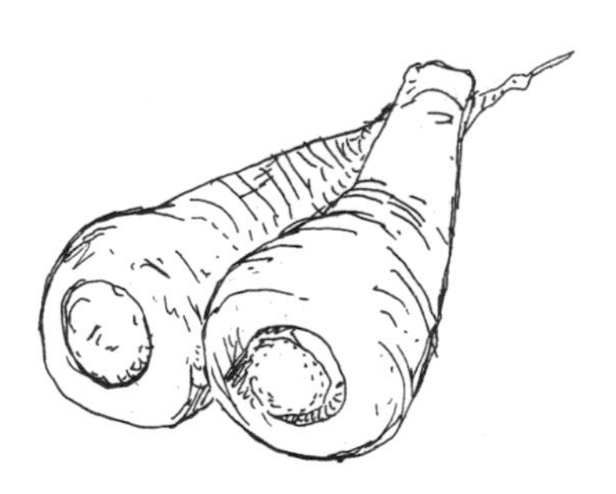

A Multitude of Main Courses

These dishes vary from the quick and easy to the more time consuming, but they are all worth the effort in the end!

The casserole type of meal improves by keeping in the refrigerator overnight, allowing the flavours to develop nicely. Most of the recipes are best not frozen as the ice tends to break up the root vegetable fibres and spoil the textures. However, they will keep for 4–5 days in the refrigerator.

I recommend Marigold vegan stock powder for flavour and content. In terms of using oils, rapeseed is light and nutritious and olive oils have wonderful flavours and goodness.

If you have people to feed who are not vegetarian, many of these dishes can be served with meat, as a vegetable side dish.

Pastry made with gluten-free flour can be very difficult to handle, but the addition of a pinch of zanthan gum makes it much easier. Don't overdue the gum or you will taste it!

Biryani

SERVES 4–6

Don't be afraid to be generous with the spices here because the rice will take up quite a bit of the flavour, especially if you cook in advance and reheat.

Rice
1 small onion, chopped
2 teaspoons sunflower oil
250g basmati rice
1 rounded teaspoon salt

1. In a 25cm fry pan, cook the onion in the oil and then add the rice.
2. Coat the rice with the onion and add 575ml of boiling water and the salt. Cover and cook gently for exactly 10 minutes.
3. Remove the lid and leave for 10 minutes. Then fluff up with a fork.

/continued

30g Pure
1 teaspoon sunflower oil
8 black peppercorns
4 cloves
2 cardamom pods, seeds removed
1 tablespoon poppy seeds
1 tablespoon fennel seeds
1 tablespoon coriander seeds
1 tablespoon cumin seeds
2 tablespoons dessicated coconut
2 medium onions, chopped
2 x 400g tins chopped tomatoes
3 cloves garlic, chopped
4cm root ginger, chopped
1 green chilli, de-seeded and chopped
8 mint leaves
4cm cinnamon stick
1 teaspoon salt
50g unsalted cashews

Sauce

1. Heat half the Pure and all of the oil in a frying pan and add the peppercorns, cloves, cardamom pods, poppy, fennel, coriander and cumin seeds, and the coconut. Fry for 2–3 minutes on a low heat. Put in a pestle and mortar and, when cool, make into a paste.

2. In another deep fry pan, heat the remaining Pure and cook the onion for about 10 minutes.

3. Stir in the tomatoes, garlic, ginger, chilli, mint and the cinnamon stick and cook for 10 minutes.

4. Turn on the oven at 180°C. Remove the cinnamon stick and purée the sauce. Now add the curry paste and salt and whizz together.

5. Roast the cashews on a baking tray in your preheated oven for 10 minutes or until golden. Leave to one side ready to scatter over the finished dish. Leave your oven turned on.

/continued

Vegetables

110g aubergines
110g carrots, peeled
110g potatoes, peeled
110g small broccoli florets
2 tablespoons olive oil
110g tinned sweet corn
110g peas
2 medium ripe tomatoes, finely sliced
Bunch of fresh coriander, chopped

1. Chop the aubergines, carrots and potatoes into 2½cm-sized chunks and scatter onto an oven tray. Add the broccoli florets. Brush with oil and roast for 25 minutes.
2. Scatter the corn and peas over the roasted vegetables. Toss into the sauce until well coated.
3. Put half the rice in a dish, spoon over the vegetable mix, and then the rest of the rice. Garnish with the tomatoes and reheat for about 20 minutes or until really hot in the middle. If you have made this dish in advance, it is best to keep the vegetable sauce and the rice separate and layer up before you are ready to put it into your oven at 200°C for about 40 minutes. I find that this prevents the sauce being absorbed too much by the rice, which makes the dish a bit stodgy.
4. Sprinkle with the chopped coriander.

MAKES 12 CAKES

Blackeyed Bean Burgers

110g blackeyed beans
110g green lentils
1 heaped teaspoon salt
1 bay leaf
Sprig of thyme
Seasoning
5 tablespoons olive oil
1 red onion, chopped
1 small leek, chopped
1 medium carrot, finely chopped
1 small red pepper, finely chopped
1 green chilli, deseeded and finely chopped
1 clove garlic, chopped
¼ teaspoon ground mace
1 teaspoon fresh thyme, chopped
1 tablespoon sundried tomato paste
2 eggs, beaten
2 tablespoons gluten-free flour

These are absolutely delicious as a supper dish but they do need the easy-to-make marmalade to complement them. These can be made in advance and kept in the refrigerator.

1. Cover the beans with water and soak overnight. Then drain.
2. Put the lentils and beans in a saucepan. Pour over 575ml water and add the salt, bay leaf and thyme. Cook until the water has been absorbed and the beans are soft. Drain any remaining liquid. Mash to a pulp and season.
3. In a large frying pan, put 1 tablespoon of olive oil and add the onion, leek, carrot, pepper, chilli and garlic. Sauté until golden brown. Add to the bean mixture along with the mace, thyme, tomato paste and 1 beaten egg. Check and adjust the seasoning.
4. Dampen your hands and form the mixture into 7½cm round cakes. Chill for at least an hour or firm up in the freezer for a while.
5. Once chilled, coat the cakes with the second beaten egg, dust with flour and using the remaining oil fry about 3 at a time for 3 minutes on each side.

Marmalade

1. Heat the oil in a saucepan and add the onions and rosemary sprigs. Cook to a golden brown and then pour in the wine and vinegar. Add the sugar and ginger. Stir and season.
2. Simmer until nearly all the liquid has gone and then remove the rosemary.

2 tablespoons olive oil
350g onions, sliced into rings
3 sprigs rosemary
270ml dry white wine
3 tablespoons white wine vinegar
2 tablespoons dark brown sugar
1 rounded dessertspoon fresh ginger root, grated
Seasoning

SERVES 4

Butterbean Cassoulet

280g butterbeans, soaked overnight in cold water
1 heaped teaspoon salt
3 tablespoons olive oil
1 large onion, sliced
1 whole bulb garlic, peeled and cloves left whole
2 medium leeks, trimmed and sliced
1 red pepper, deseeded and sliced
100g spinach, roughly chopped
100g fennel, chopped into small pieces
400g tin chopped tomatoes
575ml vegetable stock
2 sprigs fresh thyme
1 large potato
110g gluten-free breadcrumbs
2 cloves garlic, chopped
2 tablespoons parsley, chopped
2 tablespoons sunflower seeds
Seasoning

On a cold winter's evening or lunchtime, this is a fabulous dish served with some hot herby bread.

1. Rinse and drain the beans. Then put them into a saucepan, cover with water, add the salt and simmer until tender (approx. 1 hour).
2. Heat 2 tablespoons olive oil in a large saucepan over a low heat. Add the onion and fry until soft and golden.
3. Add the whole garlic cloves, leeks, pepper, spinach and fennel. Cover and fry gently for 10 minutes.
4. Add the tomatoes, butterbeans, stock and thyme. Season and simmer for 10 minutes.
5. Turn your oven on to 180°C. Peel the potato, cut into 2cm cubes and stir into the tomato mixture. Put into a large casserole, cover and place in the oven for 1–1½ hours until the butterbeans and potato are tender.
6. Turn the oven up to 200°C. In a bowl, mix together the breadcrumbs, 1 tablespoon olive oil, chopped garlic, sunflower seeds, parsley and seasoning. Scatter over the cassoulet and bake to a golden brown.

Caponata

The Sicilian vegetable stew is a real classic and I have found that the balance of richness and piquancy is just about right in this particular recipe.

SERVES 4

- 2 large aubergines, cut into cubes, salted and left to drain in a colander for about 45 minutes
- 4 plum tomatoes
- 8 tablespoons olive oil
- 1 large onion, diced into 2cm cubes
- 2 celery sticks, diced
- 1 red pepper, diced into 2cm pieces
- 2 large courgettes, cut into 1cm slices
- 50g pine nuts, toasted
- 50g capers, rinsed
- 50g green olives, roughly chopped
- Seasoning
- Good handful of basil, chopped

1. Peel and deseed the tomatoes and cut them into about 12 pieces.
2. Rinse the salted aubergines and pat dry. Sizzle them in 6 tablespoons of olive oil over a high heat and leave to drain in a colander.
3. In 2 tablespoons of oil, cook the onion and celery over a medium heat until golden brown. Add the red pepper and cook for 3 minutes. Add the courgettes and cook for a further 2 minutes.
4. Add the tomatoes and aubergines and stir in the pine nuts, capers and olives. Season well. Add the chopped basil and cook for about 5–10 minutes over a medium heat.
5. Serve with garlic bread or on a large crostini.

SERVES 4

Cashew Nut Korma

2 tablespoons rapeseed oil
2 medium onions, chopped
2 fresh green chillies, deseeded and finely chopped (3 if you like hotter curry!)
2 cloves garlic, chopped
½ teaspoon ground cumin
½ teaspoon turmeric
½ teaspoon ground coriander
125g cashew nuts, whizzed in the processor until very finely chopped
450ml tin coconut cream
½ medium cauliflower, cut into florets
110g fine beans, chopped
110g courgettes, sliced
110g frozen peas
Good handful of coriander, freshly chopped

This has proved to be one of the most popular dishes I have served at the Vale Therapy Centre and is quite quick and easy to do.

1. Heat the oil in a large saucepan over a medium heat and cook the onion until soft. Then add the chillies, garlic and spices and cook gently for 2 minutes.

2. Stir the cashews into the coconut and add the onion and chilli mixture.

3. Cook the cauliflower in salted water until just cooked but not soggy. Drain. Bring some fresh salted water to the boil and add the beans. Cook for about 5 minutes and then add the courgettes and peas. Cook for another 5 minutes and then drain well.

4. Add the cooked vegetables to the cashew and cocnut sauce. Bring up to heat and serve with basmati rice and sprinkled chopped coriander.

Chestnut and Leek Pie

SERVES 6

This pie is tasty and versatile, eaten as a main course or with salad, or as an office lunch. It keeps in the refrigerator for a good week. It is a delicious alternative meal to stuffed Turkey at Christmas time! When I was cooking for a farmer's market stall, this used to be a winner!

Pastry

335g gluten-free plain flour
Pinch of xanthan gum
Pinch of cayenne
Pinch of paprika
Salt
2 teaspoon dried mixed herbs
170 grams Pure
2 egg yolks
3 tablespoons water

Filling

55g Pure
455g leeks, sliced into 2½cm rounds
1 large onion, finely chopped
1 rounded teaspoon caraway seeds
3cm fresh ginger root, finely chopped
335g vac sealed or tinned chestnuts, chopped
4 teaspoons wholegrain mustard
Seasoning
Handful of walnuts, chopped (optional)

1. Make the pastry. Put the flour, xanthan gum, seasonings and Pure in a food processor or rub together with your fingers until it looks like golden breadcrumbs. (This golden colour indicates a nice short-crust pastry.) Add 1 egg yolk and water and bring together. Chill for at least an hour.

2. Fry the leeks gently in the Pure, with the onion and caraway seeds, until they are soft but not brown. Stir in the ginger and cook for another 2 minutes. Add the chopped chestnuts and mustard and season well.

4. Put the oven on at 180°C. Line a 20cm pie dish with half the pastry and fill with the mixture. It should be quite well mounded up in the middle. Brush the pastry edge with water, roll out the pastry lid and cover the pie. Thumb around the edge to seal well and brush with the second egg yolk. Sprinkle with chopped walnuts if desired.

5. Cook for 40 minutes or until the pastry is nicely browned.

SERVES 4

Chickpea and Spinach Curry

170g dried chickpeas, soaked overnight in cold water
1 tablespoon vegetable oil
2 teaspoons mustard seeds
55g Pure
1 large onion, sliced
3 cloves garlic, chopped
2 green chillies, deseeded and chopped
1 generous teaspoon ground cumin
1 generous teaspoon ground coriander
1 generous teaspoon ground turmeric
¼ teaspoon cayenne
425ml vegetable stock
2 x 400g tins chopped tomatoes
Seasoning
455g fresh spinach
Good handful of fresh coriander, chopped

This is a very nourishing and tasty curry.

1. Rinse and drain the chickpeas.
2. Heat the oil in a large saucepan. Add the mustard seeds and fry until they pop. Add the Pure and then the onion and cook until soft and brown.
3. Stir in the garlic, chillies and spices and cook for 1 minute. Pour in the stock and add the tomatoes and the chickpeas. Season and bring to the boil.
4. Simmer for about an hour until the chickpeas are tender. Wash the spinach and add to the pan. Season if necessary and scatter over the coriander.

Courgette and Tomato Vegetable Gratin

SERVES 9–10

At the end of the summer, when courgettes are plentiful and the tomatoes are really ripe and very red, this has to be the best dish of all! Frying the courgettes gives a wonderful flavour.

85g Pure
3 medium onions, finely chopped
3 cloves garlic, chopped
1.35kg fresh tomatoes, peeled and chopped
100g basil
9 tablespoons olive oil
2kg courgettes, chopped into rounds
225g mushrooms, roughly chopped
225g green beans, chopped and blanched
Seasoning
85g gluten-free breadcrumbs
2 tablespoons pine nuts

1. Heat the Pure in a saucepan and cook the onion and garlic for 5 minutes.
2. Add the tomatoes and cook until they have collapsed and most of the liquid has been absorbed. Add the basil.
3. Fry the courgettes in the olive oil until golden and add to the tomato mixture.
4. Fry the mushrooms and add to the dish.
5. Fold in the blanched green beans. Check for seasoning and then pile into an ovenproof dish.
6. Turn on your oven to 200°C. Top with the breadcrumbs and pine nuts and then cook for 25 minutes until golden brown and hot in the middle. Serve with some delicious hot herby or gluten-free garlic French bread and a green salad.

MAKES 8

Curried Chickpea Patties

These are simply, quite delicious. I often use them for barbecues, having pre-cooked them and kept them warm in a dish on the barbecue.

225g dried chickpeas, soaked overnight and then drained
Salt
1 small onion, peeled and chopped
1 dessertspoon lemon juice
Grated zest of ½ lemon
1 heaped teaspoon coriander seeds, roasted and cooled
1 heaped teaspoon cumin seeds, roasted and cooled
50g Pure
1 small green pepper, deseeded and chopped
2 small red chillies, deseeded and finely chopped
3 garlic cloves, chopped
1 teaspoon turmeric
10g fresh coriander
150g tinned sweet corn (drained weight)
3 tablespoons soya yogurt
1 large egg, beaten
3 tablespoons chickpea or gluten-free flour
2 tablespoons groundnut oil

1. Cover the chickpeas with water and add salt. Simmer for 30 minutes and then drain.
2. Mix the onion with the lemon juice and zest.
3. Pestle and mortar the cold roasted seeds to a powder.
4. Put the Pure in a saucepan and fry the onion, green pepper, chillies and garlic until soft and light brown. Stir in the spices and the turmeric and cook for ½ a minute.
5. Put the chickpeas in a food processor with the fresh coriander and blend until chopped but *not* puréed. A bit of texture is nice!
6. Stir in the onion mixture, sweet corn and yogurt. Mix and season well. Shape into 8 burgers (each about 1cm thick). Pop them in the freezer for about an hour so that they are easy to handle.
7. Coat each burger with egg and coat them in the flour. Heat the oil and fry in batches for about 1 minute each side. Drain and serve with salad and a nice chutney.

Honey-baked Aubergines

The different layers of flavour here, ranging from rich to sharp, make this dish really good. It can be served as a starter or as a main dish.

SERVES 6

4 aubergines, cut lengthways into thin slices

Tomato sauce

1 onion, finely chopped
2 cloves garlic, finely chopped
1 tablespoon tomato purée
400g tin chopped tomatoes
½ teaspoon cayenne pepper
2 tablespoons fresh herbs, chopped
½ tablespoon sugar

Marinade

6 tablespoons runny honey
290ml olive oil
Juice of ½ lemon
2 cloves garlic, chopped
2½ teaspoons coriander seeds, crushed
Salt and ground pepper

Sauce for topping

320ml soya single cream
3 large eggs, beaten
Juice of 1 lemon
Seasoning
2 tablespoons chives, chopped

1. First make the tomato sauce. Cook together all the ingredients in a saucepan, over a moderate heat for 15–20 minutes. Then put into a liquidiser and whizz together.
2. Combine all the marinade ingredients and whisk together with salt and ground pepper.
3. Turn the oven to 200°C and line your baking tray with Bakewell paper. Dip the aubergine slices in the marinade, shake and place on the trays. Cook for 20–30 minutes until just golden brown.
4. Meanwhile, combine the cream, eggs, lemon juice and seasoning and hand whisk until smooth.
5. Layer the aubergines, tomato sauce and cream sauce finishing with the cream sauce.
6. Bake at 180°C for approx. 20 minutes or until the cream has set. Sprinkle with chives to serve.

SERVES 4

Hot Potato Nicoise with Eggs in a Mustard Dressing

675g new potatoes (Charlotte are ideal)
Salt
Generous amount of fresh mint
4 medium eggs
110g French beans, topped, tailed and halved
110g baby broad beans
225g small vine-ripened tomatoes
4 spring onions, trimmed and sliced
4 teaspoons parsley, chopped
1 tablespoon basil, chopped

This is an ideal dish for when it is the wrong time of year for a hearty stew but not quite summery enough for a cold meal. It is also very simple to make.

1. First make the dressing. Whisk together the oil, garlic, vinegar and mustard. Then fold in the black olives.

2. Cook the potatoes in salted water with some fresh mint, until just tender. Drain and keep warm.

3. Meanwhile, bring 2 saucepans of water to the boil and put your grill on high. Hard boil the eggs in one of the saucepans for 8 minutes, remove and put to one side.

4. Put all the beans in the second pan with a little salt and cook for about 5–10 minutes, until they are only just cooked. Then drain and add them to the potatoes.

5. Cut the tomatoes in half and grill for 2 minutes, cut-side up.

6. Put the dressing in a bowl and warm over a saucepan of boiling water.
7. Add three-quarters of the warm dressing to the beans and potatoes. Add the spring onions and half the herbs, and fold over gently.
8. Peel the eggs, quarter them and then arrange on top with the tomatoes. Drizzle over the rest of the dressing. Sprinkle over the rest of the herbs.

Dressing

3 tablespoons olive oil
1 clove garlic, finely chopped
1 tablespoon white wine vinegar
2 teaspoon Dijon mustard
55g small black olives

SERVES 4

Kayi Vegetable Korma

2 tablespoons sunflower oil
1½ teaspoons black mustard seeds
2 onions, finely chopped
4 cloves garlic, chopped
3cm ginger root, peeled and grated
1–2 fresh green chillies, halved, deseeded and chopped
1 teaspoon ground coriander
½ teaspoon ground turmeric
200g tomatoes, cut into chunks
250g carrots, cut into chunks
350g potatoes, peeled and cut into chunks
250ml coconut cream
Seasoning
100g frozen peas
125g French beans
Juice of 1 lime
1 tablespoon coriander, chopped

This is a particularly nice, flavoursome curry and all of the vegetables, except for the tomatoes, can be substituted for others to suit yourself.

1. Heat the oil in a saucepan until just below smoking and add the mustard seeds. When they pop, add the onion and reduce the heat. Cook to a golden colour and then add the garlic, ginger and chillies, and cook for 5 minutes.
2. Add the coriander and turmeric and cook for 1 minute to release their fragrance. Next, add the tomatoes, carrots and potatoes and stir around. Cook to just soften the tomatoes. Add enough water to cover the vegetables and then add the coconut cream.
3. Season and simmer gently with the pan lid on to soften the vegetables. Add a little more water if you need to.
4. Add the peas and beans, turn the heat up and simmer for 5 minutes. Add the lime juice, stir around and put into your serving dish. Sprinkle over the coriander.

Majorcan Tumbet

SERVES 4

This is such a simple dish, which relies on the contrasts between the sharp tomato sauce, the rich aubergine, the crunchy peppers and the tasty fried potato layers to make it so appealing. Easy to make, it just needs a crisp green salad to make a complete meal for any time.

400g aubergines, sliced
Seasoning
4 tablespoons olive oil
400g potatoes, thinly sliced
2 red peppers, deseeded and sliced
400g tin tomatoes, chopped
1 teaspoon dried oregano
3 cloves garlic, sliced

1. Slice the aubergines, sprinkle with salt and put to drain, in a colander, for about 40 minutes.
2. Heat 2 tablespoons of olive oil in a frying pan and fry the potatoes until golden on each side. Put them in a baking dish and season.
3. Rinse the aubergines through and pat dry. Fry in a little more oil until they are brown on both sides. Place them on top of the potatoes and season.
4. Fry the red peppers and place on top of the aubergines.
5. Turn on the oven at 200°C. Over a high heat, bring together the tomatoes, oregano and garlic as a sauce. Bring to the boil and then turn down to a simmer for about 6–8 minutes.
6. Pour the sauce over the vegetables and bake for about 40 minutes until the dish is bubbling and the vegetables are tender.

MAKES 9

Millet Burgers

140g millet
500ml vegetable stock
12cm lemon grass
2cm fresh ginger root
2 tablespoons olive oil
1 red onion, chopped
1 green pepper, small, chopped
½ red pepper, small, chopped
55g pumpkin seeds, ground
1 carrot, grated
1 clove garlic, chopped
15g dried shiitake mushrooms or 55g fresh mushrooms, chopped (shiitake do give a better flavour so it is worth trying to buy them)
1 dessertspoon carob powder
2 teaspoons fresh thyme, chopped
1 dessertspoon balsamic vinegar
1 dessertspoon wheat-free soya sauce
1 teaspoon marmite
1 teaspoon dessicated coconut
2 medium eggs, beaten

1. Put the millet in a saucepan with the stock and bring to the boil. Add the lemon grass and ginger after 10 minutes. Then turn down to simmer over a low heat until all of the liquid has been absorbed.

2. Fry the onion and the green and red peppers in the olive oil until golden.

3. Discard the ginger root and lemon grass from the millet and then add the onion along with all of the other ingredients.

4. Grease a baking tray and turn the oven on to 180°C. Put spoonfuls of the burgers on the tray and flatten to about 7½cm round and 1½cm thick (be careful not to make them too thin!). Bake for about 40 minutes, turning them over half way through. They should be firm but succulent. They are delicious served with sweet and sour onion and tomato relish.

Mushroom Bhaji

SERVES 4

This is a good side dish to serve with other curries or on rice with some toasted nuts for a light meal.

3 tablespoons cooking oil
1 medium onion, chopped
3 cloves garlic, chopped
½ teaspoon turmeric
½ teaspoon chilli powder
1 teaspoon ground coriander
1 teaspoon ground cumin
¾ teaspoon salt
1 tablespoon tomato purée
250g mushrooms, cut into large slices

1. Fry the onions in the oil until they are light brown. Then lower the heat and add the garlic, turmeric, chilli, coriander and cumin. Stir and fry the spices, adding 1 tablespoon of water to prevent them from sticking. When they dry up add a little more water and do this for 5 minutes.
2. Add the salt, tomato purée and mushrooms. Add 2 tablespoons of water and simmer, covered, for 10 minutes.

SERVES 6

Mushroom, Courgette and Red Pepper Terrine

2 tablespoons roasted nuts, chopped
1 tablespoon olive oil
1 medium onion, chopped
1 clove garlic, chopped
225g mushrooms, thinly sliced
150ml vegetable stock
½ tablespoon marmite
Seasoning
280g courgettes, cut into matchsticks
1 large red pepper
3 tablespoons soya milk
3 large eggs
Good handful of basil

This very colourful and tasty terrine is so good on a buffet table with salads and hot potatoes. It is also a very good starter dish for a dinner or lunch party.

1. Line a 450kg loaf tin and dust it with some of the nuts.
2. Heat the oil in a saucepan, add the onion and garlic and cook for 3 minutes. Add the mushrooms and stock and simmer over a medium heat, uncovered, until they have absorbed all the moisture. Add the marmite and some ground black pepper and put to one side.
3. Boil the courgettes in salted water until tender and then drain and pat dry.
4. Grill and peel the red pepper and cut into strips.
5. Put the oven on to 160°C. Stir the soya milk into the mushrooms. Mix in the eggs and season well.
6. In the loaf tin, layer the mushrooms, courgettes, basil and the red pepper. Pour over the milk/egg mixture and sprinkle with the remaining nuts.

7. Bake in a bain marie for about 50–60 minutes, until firm in the middle. You can do this by half filling a baking pan with water. Then put the terrine in its loaf tin into the pan, making sure that the water does not get into the terrine.

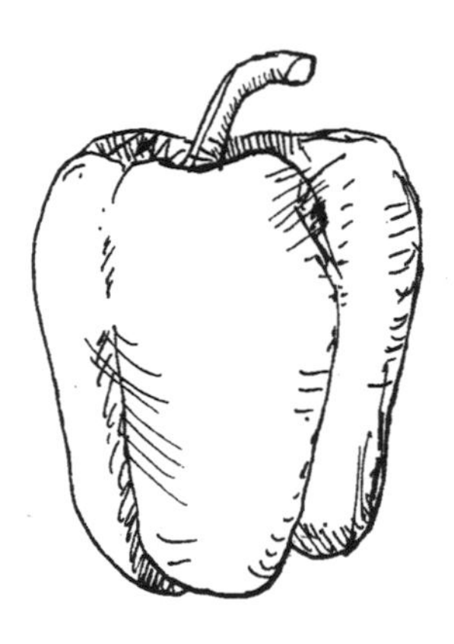

SERVES 4–6

Mushroom Korma

2 tablespoons rapeseed oil or other light oil
1 onion, chopped
2cm ginger root, grated
455g mushrooms, thickly sliced
1 red pepper, seeded and sliced
4 tablespoons Patak's Korma Paste
400g coconut milk
Squeeze of lemon juice
Pinch of sugar

This has to be the simplest, most tasty vegetarian curry ever! It is our family favourite and even the carnivores enjoy it.

1. Heat the oil, add the onion and sauté over a low heat.
2. Add the ginger, mushrooms and red pepper and cook for 5 minutes over a medium heat.
3. Add the Korma paste, coconut milk, lemon juice and sugar and simmer over a medium heat until slightly thickened and the peppers are tender. And that is it!

Mushrooms and Beans

SERVES 4

This dish has a nice zesty taste due to the white wine and sundried tomatoes. You could serve it on pasta or add a breadcrumb topping, such as the one used in the Courgette and Tomato Vegetable Gratin recipe. Alternatively, serve it on a bed of basmati rice or on a baked potato.

2 tablespoons olive oil
4 tablespoons Pure
2 shallots, chopped
680g mushrooms, sliced
3 cloves garlic, chopped
4 sundried tomatoes, chopped
6 tablespoons dry white wine
Seasoning
115g tin red kidney beans, drained and rinsed
2 tablespoons parsley, chopped

1. Put the oil and Pure in a saucepan over a medium heat and fry the shallots.
2. Add the mushrooms and garlic and fry for a few minutes.
3. Stir in the sundried tomatoes, wine, seasoning and then the beans. Cook for 5 minutes over a high heat or until most of the liquid has been absorbed. Fold in the parsley.

SERVES 6

Mushroom Tart

I am always on the look out for alternatives to quiche, which contains so much cheese and cream or milk and so are not suitable for dairy-sensitive people. This very flavoursome tart is one of my favourite recipes.

Pastry
250g gluten-free plain flour
Pinch of xanthan gum
¼ teaspoon salt
125g Pure
1 egg yolk with 1 tablespoon cold water

Filling
25g dried mushrooms
25g Pure
1 tablespoon olive oil
1 medium onion, finely chopped
450g mixed fresh mushrooms
4 tablespoons dry sherry
½ teaspoon nutmeg, freshly grated
Black pepper
2 large eggs
2 egg yolks
350ml soya milk or cream
40g walnuts, chopped
Chopped parsley to serve

1. To make the pastry, put the flour, a pinch of xanthan gum, the salt and the Pure in your food processor and whizz around until golden in colour. Add the egg yolk and water and bring together. If the pastry still seems to be too crumbly, add a little more water and whizz again. Wrap in some cling film and chill in the freezer for about 50 minutes, or put in the refrigerator for at least 2 hours.
2. Turn on your oven to 200°C. Line a 25½ x 3cm deep flan dish with greaseproof paper. Roll out the pastry and place it into the dish. Sprinkle with baking beans and bake blind for 10 minutes. Remove the beans and cook for a further 5 minutes.
3. Pour boiling water over the dried mushrooms and leave for 15 minutes.
4. Heat about one-third of the Pure and half the oil in a pan and sauté the onion until soft.

5. In another pan, put the remaining fats and sauté the fresh mushrooms. Add the sherry, nutmeg and some freshly ground black pepper and cook over a medium heat until the liquid has been absorbed.
6. Drain the dried mushrooms and mix them with the fresh mushrooms. Fold in the onions and then spread this mix over the pastry base.
7. Mix the eggs, egg yolks and soya milk or cream together. Season and pour over the mushrooms. Sprinkle over the walnuts. Cook at 180°C for about 30 minutes until firm and golden brown.
8. Serve hot or cold, sprinkled with chopped parsley.

MAKES 6

Little Lentil Pies

These little fellows are delicious to take to the office for a lunchtime snack or to serve at a picnic with a salad.

50g Puy lentils
1 dessertspoon olive oil
1 small onion, finely chopped
50g carrots, finely chopped
2 big cloves garlic, finely chopped
½ small red pepper, deseeded and finely chopped
1 ripe tomato, skinned and chopped
25g sundried tomatoes, chopped
2 teaspoons tomato purée
2 large eggs, beaten
¾ teaspoon mace, ground
Pinch of cayenne pepper
2 tablespoons mixed fresh herbs (e.g. thyme, parsley and sage), finely chopped
Seasoning

1. Cover the lentils with water and cook, covered, over a gentle heat until the liquid is absorbed and the lentils are tender. Add a little more water if necessary, towards the end of cooking. Put to one side.
2. In a small frying pan, heat the olive oil over a medium heat and cook the onion and carrot for 5 minutes. Then add the garlic and red pepper and continue cooking, stirring occasionally, until the vegetables are tender. Remove from the heat and stir in the lentils (drained if necessary), tomato, sundried tomatoes and the tomato purée.
3. Add the beaten eggs, mace, cayenne and herbs and stir around. Check for seasoning and put to one side.
4. Put the oven on at 180°C and grease a 6-cup muffin tin well with extra cooking fat.

5. To make the pastry, put the soya milk/water mix in a saucepan and bring to the boil. Put the flour in a mixing bowl and put the egg yolk into the middle. Pour over the hot fluid and mix together until a dough is formed.
6. Divide the pastry into 6 and put each ball into a muffin cup. Using your fingers, line each mould with the pastry, bringing it up the sides to just above the rims. Spoon in the mixture, filling each one right to the top. Sprinkle over the walnuts and gently press them so that they cling to the wet mixture.
7. Place the muffin tin on a baking sheet and cook the pies for 40 minutes.
8. Remove them from the oven. Carefully take the pies out of their moulds by running a knife around the insides and place them on the hot baking sheet. Cook for another 10 minutes or until the pastry is golden brown.

Pastry

25ml soya milk with 75ml water
40g vegetable fat
225g gluten-free self-raising flour
Pinch of salt and 2 large egg yolks beaten together
40g walnuts, chopped into small pieces

SERVES 6–8

Passaladiere

Pinch of xanthan gum
335g gluten-free self-raising flour
170g Pure
1 heaped teaspoon mixed Provencal herbs
Salt and pepper
1 egg yolk
3 tablespoons water
4 tablespoons olive oil
2 medium onions, sliced
2 large cloves garlic, chopped
1 tablespoon fresh thyme, chopped
1 tablespoon fresh rosemary, finely chopped
1 cup tomatoes, chopped
170g mushrooms, chopped
3 tablespoons basil, freshly chopped
2 tomatoes, sliced
10 large olives, chopped
1 tablespoon capers, washed and chopped
Parsley to sprinkle, chopped

For ages, I have been trying to make a tart that excluded all the dairy etc. Finally I alighted on a wonderous Provençal tart. The recipe included layers of grated cheese but I used chopped mushrooms and this is the delicious, rich, wonderful, herbed onion and tomato result. It can be served hot or cold, cut into squares as a cocktail nibble, as a main course and it is also wonderful for picnics.

1. Add the xanthan gum to the flour and rub in the Pure to form breadcrumbs. Add the herbs, some salt and pepper, the egg yolk and water and bring together. Chill in the refrigerator for an hour.

2. Roll out on a floured surface into a rectangle of about 30 x 40cm and transfer to a baking sheet. Alternatively, roll into a circle and line out a tart tin. The pastry needs to be about 3mm thick. Chill for about hour.

3. In a frying pan, heat 2 tablespoons of olive oil until hot. Then sauté the onion, chopped garlic, thyme, rosemary, salt and pepper. Cook over a medium heat, stirring occasionally, until really golden. This is important to really make the tart flavoursome.

4. Add the cup of tomatoes and the mushrooms and cook until all of the liquid has evaporated. Stir in the basil.

5. Put the oven on at 250°C. Brush the edges of the pastry with water and fold them over to make an edge of about 2½cm. Prick the base of the tart with a fork and pattern the edging with the fork. Put the filling into the tart and top with the slices of tomato. Brush with the remaining oil and sprinkle with olives and capers. Bake for 30–35 minutes until the pastry is golden and crisp. Sprinkle with some chopped parsley and enjoy!

SERVES 4–6

Red Kidney Bean Hot Pot

110g dried kidney beans
30g Pure
1 onion, chopped
110g celery, sliced
110g carrots, sliced
1 tablespoon gluten-free flour
300ml vegetable stock
Seasoning
Good handful of fresh parsley, chopped
110g runner beans, sliced
110g courgettes, sliced

Topping
200g gluten-free wholemeal breadcrumbs
100g walnuts, chopped
1 tablespoon sunflower seeds
1 tablespoon pumpkin seeds

This is such a good warming dish for the autumn when the runner beans are on the wane but the courgettes are still plentiful.

1. First cook the kidney beans. Place them in a saucepan and cover generously with water. Bring to the boil and then simmer gently for 1½ hours, skimming off water if necessary. The kidney beans should be tender so cook for a little more or less as necessary.
2. Melt the Pure, add the onion and fry for 5 minutes.
3. Add the celery and carrots. Cook gently with the lid on. Take off of the heat and blend in the flour.
4. Add the stock gradually, stirring all the time to keep a smooth sauce. Simmer and season. At this stage a handful of fresh parsley will lend some interest and flavour. Add the runner beans and the courgettes.
5. Drain the kidney beans and add to the vegetables.

6. Combine the topping ingredients. Put the casserole in a serving dish and sprinkle over the topping. You can now leave your casserole to one side until you are ready to cook and eat it.
7. Preheat the oven to 190°C about 15 minutes before you are ready to heat the casserole, and then cook for about 40 minutes or until it is really hot in the middle.

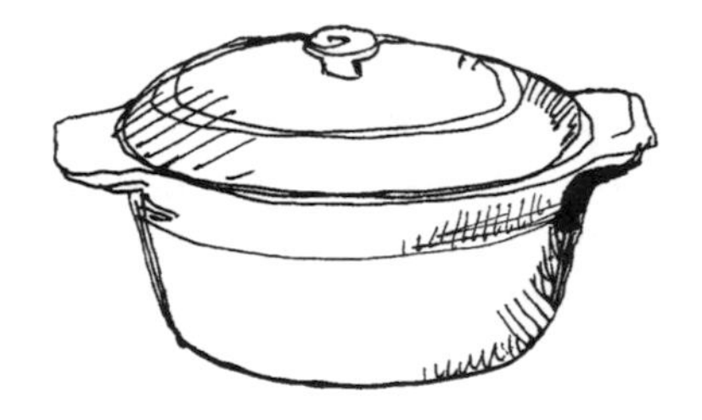

SERVES 8

Red Pepper Empanada

350g plain gluten-free flour
Pinch of xanthan gum
175g Pure
Salt
1 teaspoon mixed dried herbs
1 egg blended with 4–5 tablespoons cold water
2 tablespoons olive oil
1 onion, finely chopped
1 red pepper, finely chopped
500g potatoes, peeled and diced into small pieces
300ml dry cider or white wine
2 tablespoons tomato purée
1 tablespoon parsley, chopped
1 teaspoon dried or 2 teaspoons fresh thyme
½ dessertspoon smoked paprika (or more if you like things really fiery)
225g mushrooms, roughly chopped or 200g vacuum-packed chestnuts, roughly chopped
1 egg yolk mixed with 2 tablespoons soya milk

Empanada is Northern Spain's answer to our Cornish pasty. It is usually quite fiery with the smoked paprika and it includes some form of fish, for example tuna. This version is made as a pie because I find that the gluten-free flour is not easy to form into a pasty, and I have substituted the fish with mushrooms but you could also use cooked chestnuts.

1. First make the pastry. Put the flour, xanthan gum, Pure, ½ teaspoon of salt and mixed herbs in your processor and whizz until it resembles golden breadcrumbs. Add the egg and water and whizz to bring together. Wrap in cling film and refrigerate for a couple of hours or pop it into the freezer for an hour.

2. Heat the oil over a medium heat and cook the onion, red pepper and potato for about 10 minutes, stirring, until the vegetables are just cooked.

3. Add the cider or white wine, tomato purée, parsley, thyme and paprika. Allow to bubble and simmer for 10 minutes. Taste and add salt and more paprika if you like.

4. Remove from the heat. Fry the mushrooms in a little Pure and then fold them in. If you are using chestnuts, fold them in instead. Leave to cool.
5. Preheat the oven to 180°C. Line a 20 x 4cm pie dish with two-thirds of the pastry. Pile in the mixture, brush the edge with water, and roll the rest of the pastry over the mixture. Crimp around the edges of the pie, brush with a little egg/soya milk mixture and cook at 180°C until golden (30–40 minutes).
6. Delicious served hot with green beans or cold with a green salad and Green Bean Chutney.

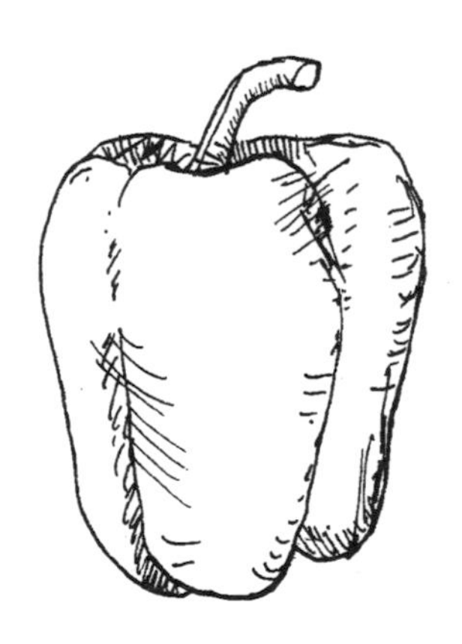

SERVES 4

Root Vegetable and Nut Crumble

170g potatoes
170g carrots
170g parsnips
170g swede
170g butternut squash
170g chestnut mushrooms
30g Pure
2 leeks, trimmed and sliced
1 teaspoon paprika
30g gluten-free wholemeal flour
300ml vegetable stock
400g tin chopped tomatoes
150ml soya milk

Topping
170g gluten-free wholemeal flour
115g Pure
40g mixed nuts, chopped
1 tablespoon pumpkin seeds
1 tablespoon sunflower seeds
2 tablespoons parsley, chopped
Salt and pepper

This is a really wholesome country dish that is very welcome and comforting on a cold winter's day when you need nurturing! Be generous with your seasoning and herbs.

1. Peel and chop the vegetables into 2½cm chunks and rough chop the mushrooms.
2. Melt the Pure, add the leeks and cook over a medium heat until tender.
3. Add the root vegetables and mushrooms, cover and cook over a low heat for 10 minutes.
4. Stir in the paprika and flour and then gradually add the stock, stirring all the time to keep the sauce smooth. Then add the tomatoes. Cover and simmer until the vegetables are tender.
5. Remove from the heat and fold in the soya milk.
6. Put the oven on at 200°C and make the topping. Crumble the flour and Pure together by hand, and stir in the nuts, seeds, parsley and some salt and pepper.
7. Check the seasoning in the vegetables, then put into your dish and cover with the crumble. Cook for about 40 minutes until golden brown and then enjoy!

Spicy Spinach and Kidney Bean Cakes

SERVES 4

I went to a buffet lunch and homed in on a dish of these delicious savoury cakes which were made quite small and served as finger food. They were so good, I came home with the recipe!

- 1 tablespoon groundnut oil
- 1 green chilli, seeded and chopped
- 350g frozen spinach, chopped
- Seasoning
- ¼ teaspoon nutmeg, grated
- ¼ teaspoon cayenne pepper
- ¼ teaspoon ground cinnamon
- 400g tin red kidney beans, drained
- 65g gluten-free breadcrumbs
- Grated rind of 1 lemon
- Good pinch of smoked paprika
- 1 egg, beaten

1. Heat 1 teaspoon of the oil in a small frying pan and fry the chilli for a minute. Add the frozen spinach, cover and cook for 5 minutes, until soft.
2. Season and stir in the nutmeg, cayenne and cinnamon. Simmer until all of the liquid has evaporated. Leave to cool slightly.
3. Mash the kidney beans in a bowl with a fork and then stir in the spinach mixture.
4. Shape into 16 cakes (or smaller if they are for a finger buffet) with floured hands. Leave them to cool in the freezer until firm.
5. Mix together the breadcrumbs, lemon rind and paprika.
6. Gently brush the cakes with the egg and dip them in the crumbs to coat them completely.
7. Heat the remaining oil in a non-stick frying pan and fry a few cakes at a time, on both sides, for about 5 minutes, until golden brown.

SERVES 4 MAIN COURSE
OR 8 FOR BUFFET

2 tablespoons olive oil
1 medium red onion, chopped
3 plump cloves garlic, finely chopped
25g pine nuts
250g spinach, washed
3 large eggs
2 heaped tablespoons sage, chopped
Salt and pepper
Pinch of ground nutmeg

Spinach Frittata

I found this recipe in our village cookery book. It is so easy to do in the oven and that is good news if you want to be getting on with something else. You will need a 20cm loose-bottomed cake tin for this recipe.

1. Line the cake tin with Bakewell paper.
2. Heat the olive oil gently and fry the onion and garlic until soft. Add the pine nuts and put to one side.
3. Cook the spinach in a saucepan in its own moisture until wilted. Drain and squeeze dry and add to the onion mixture.
4. Turn on your oven to 200°C. Whisk the eggs well and add the herbs, salt, pepper and nutmeg and pour into the lined tin. Cook for about 25 minutes until really firm in the middle.

Toasted Hazelnut Burgers

These are fantastic for a barbeque or hog roast when a vegetarian option is required. They also freeze well either uncooked or cooked.

MAKES 6

85g hazelnuts, toasted
2 medium carrots, grated
2 celery stalks, finely chopped
1 medium onion, finely chopped
2 tablespoons parsnip, grated
150g frozen peas, defrosted
2 tablespoons spinach, chopped
2 tablespoons gluten-free breadcrumbs
1 tablespoon parsley, finely chopped
2 pinches of cayenne
1 pinch of mace
1 large egg
1 tablespoon tomato purée
1 tablespoon soya yogurt

Coating
1 large egg, beaten
85g gluten-free breadcrumbs

Salsa (optional)
1 small fresh green chilli, chopped
1 small red pepper, seeded and chopped
½ small red onion, chopped
2 tablespoons coriander, chopped
Juice of 1 lime
1 large tomato, skinned, deseeded and chopped

1. Whizz the nuts to a powder. Add the vegetables, breadcrumbs, parsley and spices and mix well.
2. In another bowl whisk together the egg, tomato purée and yogurt and add to the vegetables.
3. Make into 6 burgers and put into the freezer for 1 hour or until they are easy to pick up. Preheat your oven to 180°C about 15 minutes before you are ready to cook.
4. Dip the burgers in the beaten egg and coat with the crumbs. Cook for about 15 minutes on each side.
5. You can also freeze these burgers, defrost them in your refrigerator and reheat in a pre-heated oven at 180°C for about 25 minutes.
6. Serve with a good chutney or make the tasty salsa to go with them. Put all the salsa ingredients into your liquidiser and just whizz to a finely chopped consistency.

SERVES 4

Vegetable Bhaji

3 tablespoons cooking oil
½ teaspoon black mustard seeds
½ teaspoon ground cumin
2 whole red dried chillies
4 cloves garlic, chopped
½ teaspoon chilli powder
115g carrots
115g green beans
230g potatoes
115g onions, finely shredded
1 teaspoon salt
2 tablespoons fresh coriander, chopped

I find this an excellent side dish to go with kormas. It is quite fiery but the contrast with the creamy korma is good.

1. Heat the oil in a saucepan over a high heat and add the mustard seeds, cumin and chillies. Stir and then add the garlic and chilli powder and cook for a couple of minutes.

2. Cut the vegetables into matchsticks and add them along with the onions and the salt to the pan. Cover and cook for about 20–25 minutes on a low heat until just tender. Sprinkle with the chopped coriander.

Vegetable Bourguignon with Chestnuts

SERVES 4

The chestnuts give this warming casserole an almost 'meaty' texture. I find that chestnuts are a far, far nicer alternative to meat than any of the so-called meat substitutes which are found in the supermarkets. If you would like it to be more robust, use more red wine and less vegetable stock!

30g Pure
1 large onion, chopped
4 cloves garlic, chopped
455g carrots, sliced
4 large sticks celery, sliced
455g leeks, thickly chopped
225g button mushrooms
2 bay leaves
2 tablespoons gluten-free flour
500ml red wine
800ml vegetable stock
335g vac sealed or tinned chestnuts
Salt and pepper
Good handful of parsley, chopped

1. Melt the Pure in a large heavy saucepan and add the onion. Cook for 5 minutes.
2. Add the garlic, carrots, celery, leeks, mushrooms and bay leaves. Stir and cook for 5 minutes.
3. Sprinkle the flour over the vegetables and stir over the heat for 2 minutes. Pour in the wine slowly, stirring all the time to keep the sauce smooth. Add the stock and bring to the boil and then simmer gently until the vegetables are just tender – they do need a bit of texture.
4. Roughly chop the chestnuts and add to the hot pot. Season and sprinkle well with parsley. Serve with hot French gluten-free bread or dip some wholemeal bread into the stew. Lovely!

SERVES 4 OR 8 FOR BUFFET

Vegetable Frittata

115g carrots, cut into 2½cm strips
115g red onion, chopped
115g courgette, cut into 2½cm strips
115g mangetout, cut into 3 crossways
4 very large eggs
Salt and pepper
1 heaped tablespoon parsley, chopped
1 tablespoon pine nuts
A little Pure or olive oil

This is the perfect fodder for a picnic!

1. Boil 5cm of water in a saucepan. Salt and add the carrots and onions and cook for 2 minutes.

2. Add the courgette and cook for another minute. Add the mangetout and cook for 1 minute. Drain the vegetables well.

3. Put the grill on hot. Whisk together the eggs and salt and pepper and add some of the parsley. Put a little Pure or some olive oil into an 18cm non-stick fry pan and add the vegetables and pine nuts over a high heat. Pour over the eggs.

4. Move the frittata around with a palette knife until all of the egg is just cooked and the bottom is set. Put the pan under the grill and brown the top of the frittata. Turn over onto a serving dish and sprinkle with some more parsley. Serve warm.

Vegetable Moussaka

SERVES 8

600ml vegetable stock
110g Puy lentils
110g green lentils
8 tablespoons olive oil
4 medium onions, chopped
4 large red peppers, chopped
4 cloves garlic, chopped
900g aubergines, diced to 2cm, salted and put to drain in a colander
2 x 400g tins chopped tomatoes
400ml red wine
4 tablespoons tomato purée
2 teaspoons ground cinnamon
140g courgettes, roughly chopped
4 tablespoons parsley, chopped

Sauce
55g Pure
55g gluten-free flour
600ml soya cream or milk
½ teaspoon nutmeg, grated
2 large eggs, beaten
Juice of 1 lemon
Salt and pepper

This moussaka is delicious – far nicer than any meat moussaka that I have ever come across.

1. Put the stock in a large saucepan with the Puy lentils and simmer for 15 minutes. Add the green lentils and cook for a further 15 minutes until soft.
2. Heat 2 tablespoons of oil in a large saucepan and fry the onions, peppers and garlic.
3. Wash the drained aubergines, pat dry and fry in a separate frying pan until golden.
4. Drain the tomatoes and add them, the lentils and aubergines to the fried vegetables.
5. Mix the wine, tomato purée and cinnamon and pour over the vegetables. Add the courgettes. Cook gently for about 10 minutes to bring everything together. Fold in the parsley. Put into a large serving/ baking dish.
6. To make the sauce, melt the Pure in a saucepan. Add the flour and cook for 2 minutes. Remove from the heat and pour in the cream or milk, slowly, whisking all the time. Add the grated nutmeg and whisk together until smooth.
7. Put your oven on at 180°C. Add the beaten eggs, lemon juice, salt and pepper and whisk together again. Spread over the moussaka base and bake until the sauce has set and is golden brown.

SERVES 5

Vegetable Cottage Pie

110g black-eyed beans, pre-soaked overnight
85g split peas, rinsed
85g green lentils, rinsed
700ml vegetable stock
450g parsnips
450g potatoes
110g Pure
Salt and pepper
55g carrots, finely chopped
55g swede, finely chopped
55g celeriac, finely chopped
1 large onion, chopped
1 small red pepper, finely chopped
100g frozen peas, defrosted
225g tomatoes, sliced
1 heaped tablespoon fresh herbs, chopped
¼ teaspoon ground nutmeg
¼ teaspoon cayenne pepper

This recipe freezes well so make several small pies and use whenever convenient.

1. Drain the black-eyed beans and put them in a saucepan with the split peas and lentils. Add the stock and simmer, covered, for 50–60 minutes. The pulses should be soft but not over dry. If they are too dry, add a little more stock. Mash them a little with a fork but still retain some texture.
2. Cook the potatoes and parsnips together in salted water. Drain and mash with 50g of Pure and some ground pepper.
3. Melt 50g of Pure in a large frying pan and cook the carrots, swede, celeriac, onion and red pepper very gently until soft. Stir in the peas.
4. Skin the tomatoes by pouring over boiling water and leaving to stand for a couple of minutes. Then peel and slice thickly.

5. Put your oven on at 180°C. Mix the pulses, cooked vegetables, herbs and spices together and taste and season. Put these into your pie dish, layer the tomatoes over and then put the potato mix on top. Brush with the remaining melted Pure and heat through in the oven.

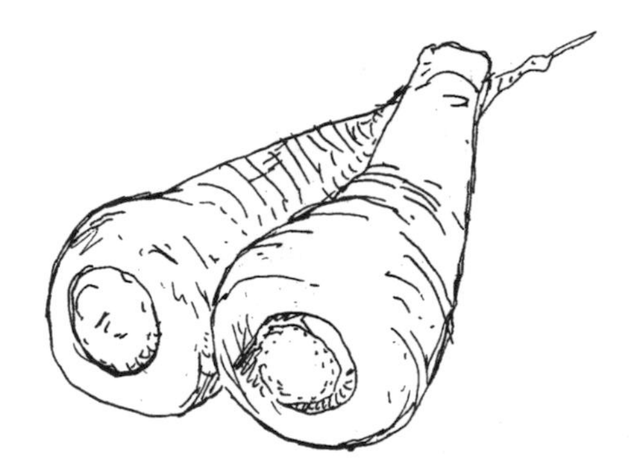

SERVES 4 GENEROUSLY

Vegetable Tagine

2 tablespoons olive oil
1 large onion, peeled and sliced
2 cloves garlic, chopped
1 teaspoon ground cumin
1 teaspoon ground cinnamon
1 teaspoon ground ginger
1 medium aubergine, cut into 4cm chunks
1 teaspoon saffron strands
2 x 400g tins chopped tomatoes
1½ tablespoons clear honey
½–1 teaspoon harissa paste
85g dried apricots, chopped
1 cinnamon stick
Peel of 1 lemon, cut into strips
½ teaspoon salt
110g butternut squash, cut into 4cm chunks
110g turnips, cut into 4cm chunks
250g chestnut mushrooms, quartered
55g whole blanched almonds
1 tablespoon preserved lemon, chopped

This is so tasty – just be careful not to overcook the vegetables.

1. Heat the oil in a large saucepan and add the onion. Cook for 10 minutes over a medium heat, covered. Add the garlic and spices and cook for 2 minutes.
2. Add the aubergine and cook for 5 minutes.
3. Stir in the saffron, tomatoes, honey and harissa paste (this is quite hot stuff so add according to your palate!).
4. Add the apricots, cinnamon stick, lemon peel and salt. Stir in the squash, turnips and mushrooms and bring to the boil. Turn down to simmer, covered, until the vegetables are only just tender. Do not let the vegetables go to a mush!
5. Scatter over the almonds and chopped preserved lemon. If possible, leave to stand for a while, or overnight, in the refrigerator to allow the flavours to develop.

CHAPTER 4

A Temptation of Terrines and Stuffed Vegetables

These dishes are very versatile and are delicious as a starter, main course, picnic food or buffet any time of the year. To really make them extra good, it is important to use fresh herbs rather than dried for real flavour and oomph. You also need to be generous with spices and freshly milled black pepper.

SERVES 6 MAIN COURSE

Baby Aubergines Stuffed with Mushrooms and Nuts

6 baby aubergines
1 tablespoon olive oil
1 medium onion, chopped
1 clove garlic, chopped
110g button mushrooms, chopped
150g fine beans, blanched and chopped
195g tin sweet corn, drained
30g pine nuts
Ground black pepper
2 tablespoons thyme, chopped
2 tomatoes, skinned and chopped
2 tablespoons parsley, chopped

The richness of the aubergines and the sharpness of the tomatoes combined with the other ingredients makes this really special.

1. Put your oven on at 180°C. Halve the aubergines and put them in a saucepan. Cover with water, add salt and cook for 5 minutes until just tender. Scoop out the flesh and chop this up. Put the aubergine skins to one side.

2. Put the oil in a frying pan and on a medium heat cook the onion, covered, for 5 minutes. Stir in the aubergine flesh, garlic, mushrooms, beans, corn, pine nuts, ground black pepper, thyme and tomatoes. Fold in the parsley.

3. Put the aubergine skins into a greased baking dish and fill with the mixture. Bake for 15 minutes. Serve on their own or with a fresh tomato sauce.

Cashew Nut and Broccoli Roulade

SERVES 6

This unusual roulade is a very nice combination of textures and taste and is good for a starter, on a buffet or for a light meal.

200g roasted unsalted cashew nuts
2 cloves garlic, chopped
4 large eggs
Salt and pepper
2–3 tablespoons mayonnaise
455g broccoli
2 tablespoons chives
1 lemon

1. Turn the oven on to 200°C and line a 23 x 33cm Swiss roll tin with Bakewell paper.
2. Put the nuts and garlic in a food processor and whizz to a fine breadcrumb consistency.
3. Whisk the eggs and seasoning until very thick and leaving a trail.
4. Stir two-thirds of the nuts, very gently, into the eggs and spread in the tin. Bake until just firm – about 8 minutes.
5. Sprinkle some Bakewell paper with the remaining cashews and turn the roulade over onto the paper. Leave to cool.
6. Break the broccoli into florets and cook in boiling salted water until just tender. Cool.
7. Spread the roulade with the mayonnaise, sprinkle over the chives and broccoli and roll up from the narrow end. Use your fingers to tuck the end of the roulade firmly under at the beginning of the roll and keep firmly tucking in to give a nicely shaped roll. Serve with lemon mayonnaise.

SERVES 6

Cashew Nut and Sundried Tomato Terrine

2 tablespoons sundried tomato oil (from a jar of sundried tomatoes)
1 large onion, finely chopped
2 cloves garlic, finely chopped
400g tin tomatoes, drained and chopped
12 sundried tomatoes, finely chopped
200g cashew nuts, finely chopped (or processed not too finely)
1 grated lemon rind
2 tablespoons basil, chopped
2 eggs
Salt and black pepper

Whenever I am asked to cook for a buffet this is always the terrine that is most enjoyed and commented upon. You can freeze it, so you could slice it up and take out a piece anytime to take to the office for lunch.

1. Put your oven on at 180°C. Gently heat the oil in a deep frying pan. Add the onion and garlic and cook for 5 minutes.
2. Add the tinned tomatoes and cook until the liquid has completely evaporated.
3. Remove from the heat and stir in the cashew nuts, sundried tomatoes, lemon rind, basil, eggs and plenty of salt and black pepper.
4. Line a 455g loaf tin with Bakewell paper and pile the mixture in. Cook for 45–60 minutes until firm and slightly blackened to bring out the flavour. Serve cold with pesto mayonnaise.

Courgettes Stuffed with Lentil and Walnut Pâté

SERVES 4

Vegan food is not always very flavoursome but this combination of ingredients really seems to work – just be generous with your measuring of ingredients. I also use this pâté as a topping on bruschetta for cocktail parties.

110g red lentils
½ onion, chopped
1 clove garlic, chopped
250ml vegetable stock
30g walnuts, chopped
2 teaspoons cider vinegar
2 teaspoons Marmite
2 dessertspoons dates, chopped
1 tablespoon rapeseed oil
1 teaspoon soya milk
3 teaspoons thyme, chopped
Seasoning
4 courgettes
1 tablespoon wheat-free soy sauce
1 tablespoon olive oil

1. Put your oven on at 180°C. Cover the lentils with water in a saucepan and bring to the boil. Then drain.
2. Return them to the saucepan and add the onion, garlic and vegetable stock. Bring to the boil and then simmer for 20 minutes.
3. Drain and stir in the rest of the ingredients except for the courgettes. Whizz in a food processor until you reach the consistency that you prefer. I think that it is best slightly on the rough side. Season well.
4. Slice a sliver off the base of each courgette so that it sits nicely. Also cut a rectangle out of the top of each one and then carefully scoop out the flesh.
5. Mix together the soy sauce and olive oil and brush the cut surfaces of the courgettes. Bake for 15 minutes.
6. Now fill the courgettes with the pâté and heat through for 10 minutes. Serve hot or cold with red onion marmalade.

SERVES 6

Curried Nut Terrine

1 tablespoon olive oil
2 medium onions, chopped
1 green pepper, chopped
1 small leek, finely chopped
225g walnuts
85g gluten-free breadcrumbs
1 clove garlic, chopped
1 heaped tablespoon parsley, freshly chopped
1 heaped tablespoon thyme, freshly chopped
1 teaspoon curry powder
225g fresh tomatoes, peeled and chopped
2 large eggs
Seasoning

I like this served with homemade green bean chutney and a crispy green salad. You can also serve it hot with stuffed tomatoes or a rich tomato sauce. Nut roast is so maligned yet this tastes so good!

1. Over a gentle heat fry the onions, pepper and leek in a little olive oil until soft.
2. Put the nuts and breadcrumbs in your food processor and mix well. Put into a bowl.
3. Add the garlic, herbs and curry powder to the nut mix.
4. Now, combine the onion and nut mixes and fold in the tomatoes. Bind together with the eggs and season nicely.
5. Put your oven on at 170°C and line a 450g loaf tin with Bakewell paper. Pack the mixture in and bake until firm. Serve hot with a tomato sauce or cold with salad as a picnic. Either way it is delicious.

Stuffed Mushrooms

SERVES 2

Life is definitely not too short to stuff these mushrooms! The lime juice and fruit version is nicely citrusy in the richness of the mushroom, and the vegetable version is equally good. This can be served as a main course by slicing the mushrooms, layering them in a dish and then putting the filling over, as a topping, before baking in the oven. Serve with a good crisp salad and hot bread. Divine!

2 large mushrooms
2 tablespoons olive oil
2 spring onions, chopped
½ red pepper or 4 dried apricots, chopped
1 small courgette or sour apple, chopped
4 black olives, chopped
2 tablespoons oats or quinoa flakes if you are gluten free
1 tablespoon basil, chopped
1 tablespoon wheat-free soy sauce
1 tablespoon lime juice
Seasoning
1 tablespoon chives, chopped

1. Put the oven on to 180°C. Remove the mushroom stalks and chop them. In a pan, heat the olive oil on a medium heat and cook the stalks, onions, peppers (or apricots), courgette (or apple), olives, oats (or quinoa) until the oats are golden brown.
2. Stir in the basil, soy sauce, and lime juice and season well.
3. Oil the mushrooms, sprinkle with salt and ground black pepper and fill with the stuffing. Bake for 15–20 minutes.
4. Sprinkle with the chopped chives.

SERVES 6

Spinach Roulade

15g Pure
55g walnuts, finely chopped
455g fresh spinach, washed
4 large eggs, separated
¼ nutmeg, freshly grated
Salt and pepper
2–3 tablespoons mayonnaise
3 tomatoes, chopped or 1 large red pepper, roasted and skinned
2 tablespoons chives, chopped

This delicious roulade was served at a lunch party years ago and my hostess gave me the recipe. It has never gone out of fashion and I still get nice comments about it.

1. Put your oven on at 200°C and line a 23 x 33cm Swiss roll tin with Bakewell paper. Grease the paper with some Pure and sprinkle with some of the walnuts.
2. Cook the spinach in its own moisture until wilted. Drain and squeeze hard until all the moisture has gone.
3. Put the spinach, the rest of the Pure, egg yolks, nutmeg, salt and pepper in your food processor and whizz until blended.
4. In another bowl, whisk the egg whites until stiff and fold gently into the spinach mixture until absorbed. Spread over the baking tin and cook until just firm (about 8–10 minutes).
5. Put the remaining walnuts on a large piece of Bakewell paper and turn the roulade over onto the nuts and leave to cool.

6. Spread thc mayonnaise over the roulade. Sprinkle over the tomatoes or pepper and the chives. Roll up the roulade from the narrow end, tucking the end firmly in to start the roll. Using the paper to help you, keep a tight roll by using your fingers to keep the roulade compact. Leave wrapped in the paper in the refrigerator until ready to eat.
7. Turn out onto your serving dish and serve with some more mayonnaise with chives.

SERVES 6

The Vale Terrine

450ml vegetable stock
85g green or yellow split peas
55g Puy Lentils
55g green lentils
55g Pure
85g onions, finely chopped
1 carrot, finely chopped
1 stick celery, finely chopped
1 small leek, finely chopped
1 medium courgette, chopped
½ red pepper, finely chopped
50g spinach
1 clove garlic, finely chopped
Pinch of cayenne
Pinch of mace
1 large egg
2 tablespoons parsley, chopped
Seasoning

I invented this terrine to serve at the Vale Centre in Somerset where they let me loose (in a culinary sort of way!) with their students as regards their lunchtime food. It is packed full of goodness and taste and lends itself well as a part of a buffet lunch.

1. Bring the stock to the boil in a saucepan, add the split peas and Puy lentils and simmer for 5 minutes.
2. Add the green lentils and simmer, with the lid on, for 25 minutes or until they are soft and the liquid has been absorbed. Put the oven on at 180°C.
3. Gently heat the Pure in a frying pan on a low heat and add the vegetables and garlic. Fry until soft and golden.
4. Stir in the pea and lentil mix, cayenne, mace, egg and parsley.
5. Check the seasoning. Put into a 450g Bakewell paper-lined loaf tin and cook until firm – about 40 minutes.

Tomato, Courgette and Red Pepper Terrine

SERVES 6

This recipe is based on the mushroom terrine for those who are unable to eat mushrooms. It is very attractive on a buffet or as a starter.

- 2 tablespoons roasted nuts, finely chopped
- 1 tablespoon olive oil
- 1 clove garlic, chopped
- 1 onion, chopped
- 400g tin tomatoes, chopped
- 280g courgettes, cut into matchsticks
- 1 large red pepper
- 3 tablespoons soya milk
- 1 tablespoon sundried tomato paste
- 3 large eggs
- Salt and pepper
- Basil leaves

1. Grease and line a 455g loaf tin and dust with some of the nuts.
2. Gently heat the oil in a saucepan on a low heat and add the garlic and onion. Cook for 2 minutes and then pour in the tomatoes. Cook uncovered to reduce, until the liquid has evaporated.
3. Meanwhile, boil the courgettes in salt water until tender. Drain and pat dry.
4. Grill the red pepper and peel and cut into strips.
5. Put the oven on at 160°C. Mix together the tomato mixture, soya milk and eggs and season well.
6. Layer the tomato mixture, courgettes, basil leaves and red pepper. Sprinkle with the remaining nuts and bake in a bain marie for 50–60 minutes until firm in the middle. (You can do this by placing the terrine in its loaf tin into a deep baking dish and pouring cold water into the dish until it is half way up the terrine.)

SERVES 4 FOR MAIN COURSE
OR 8 FOR BUFFET

Vegetables Stuffed with Risotto

30g Pure
140g risotto rice
2 baby leeks, chopped
150ml dry white wine
600ml vegetable stock
110g button mushrooms, chopped
1 small courgette, chopped
55g mixed nuts, chopped
Good handful of fresh herbs (e.g. mint, parsley, marjoram)
Seasoning
4 beef tomatoes
4 red, yellow or green peppers
Walnut oil to drizzle

These are so easy to do and to keep warm, so if you have a supper party going on they are really hassle free. Also, if some of your guests prefer to eat meat, they make an ideal accompaniment to such things as chicken breasts or gammon.

1. Heat the Pure in a deep frying pan on a medium heat, add the rice and cook for 3 minutes.
2. Add the leeks and cook for 2–3 minutes. Pour over the wine and allow to bubble up and then add ¼ of the stock and cook on a medium heat until absorbed.
3. Add the remaining stock a little at a time and cook gently until the rice is tender – about 20 minutes. Add more stock if necessary to complete the process.
4. Mix the rice with the chopped mushrooms, courgettes and nuts. A handful of mixed fresh herbs will add to the flavour so add them now. Check the seasoning and add more if necessary.

5. Put your oven on at 190°C. Slice the tops off the beef tomatoes and scoop out the insides. Slice the tops off the peppers and de-seed them and put these vegetables in a greased baking dish. Fill them with the risotto, place the tops back on and drizzle with walnut oil.
6. Bake for 20–25 minutes until they are tender but still firm.

SERVES 4 MAIN COURSE
OR 8 FOR BUFFET

Turkish Stuffed Tomatoes

- 1 dessertspoon, toasted sesame oil
- 1 small onion, peeled and chopped
- 1 clove garlic, chopped
- 150ml risotto rice
- 1 heaped teaspoon ground cinnamon
- 1 tablespoon pine nuts
- 1 tablespoon chopped apricots
- Seasoning
- 300ml vegetable stock
- 2 teaspoons fresh thyme, chopped
- 30g walnuts, chopped
- 8 beef tomatoes (large slicing tomatoes)
- 2 teaspoons golden caster sugar

I love the way the thyme and cinnamon flavours come through in this dish. Serve on a bruscetta rubbed with garlic to make a good first course.

1. Heat the sesame oil in a deep fry pan on a low heat and fry the onion until soft. Then add the garlic and dry rice.
2. Add the cinnamon, pine nuts and apricots and stir until well coated. Season with salt and freshly ground black pepper and pour over the stock. Stir once, then cover the pan and simmer on a low heat for 15–20 minutes. The liquid should then be absorbed and the rice tender.
3. Remove from the heat, add the thyme and fluff up with a fork and add the walnuts.
4. Put the oven on at 180°C and slice the stalk end off the tomatoes and keep. Scoop out the core and seeds but leave the side flesh. Put a pinch of sugar into each tomato and then pack in the rice mixture and put the lids back on.
5. Put the tomatoes in a roasting pan with a little water. Sprinkle with salt and pepper. Drizzle with olive oil and bake for 25–30 minutes, until just cooked. Serve hot or cold.

CHAPTER 5

A Pride of Potatoes

The great chip alternative! Varied. Quick. Easy!

MAKES 8 CAKES

Courgette and Potato Cakes

335g courgettes
Salt
335g Desiree potatoes, left unpeeled
2 cloves garlic, finely chopped
2 spring onions, finely chopped
2 tablespoons mint, freshly chopped
1 large egg
1 tablespoon gluten-free flour
1 tablespoon olive oil
30g Pure

These sound a great fiddle to do, but are in fact quite easy – and just so good to eat with any of the salads or main courses.

1. Coarsely grate the courgettes, sprinkle with salt and put them into a colander to drain. Leave for about an hour and then rinse through with water.
2. Par-boil the potatoes in their jackets for 8 minutes and leave to cool. Peel the potatoes and grate coarsely.
3. Put the rinsed courgettes in a clean tea towel, wrap up like a cracker and squeeze all the moisture out. They do need to be as dry as possible.
4. Then mix together the potatoes, courgettes, garlic, spring onions, mint and egg and lightly toss together with two forks. Divide the mixture into 8 and flour your work surface.
5. Shape the cakes into rounds about 2cm thick and lightly dust with flour.

6. Put the oven on at 220°C and pre-heat a baking sheet. Melt the oil and Pure together, brush the cakes on both sides and place on the baking sheet.
7. Cook on the top rack for 15 minutes and then on the middle rack for another 10–15 minutes. Serve warm.

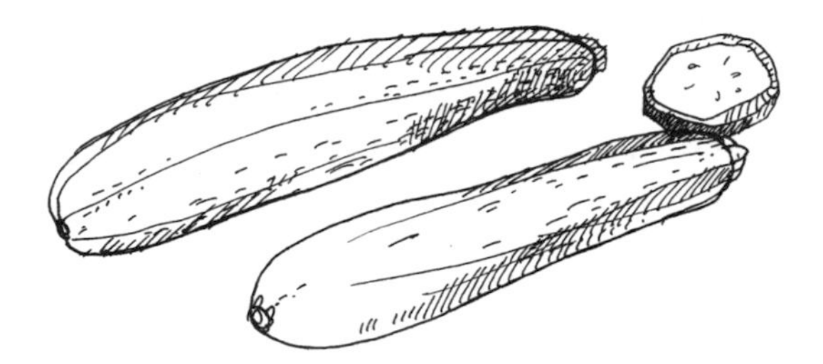

SERVES 4

Chilli Potatoes

600g potatoes, peeled and cut into 2cm chunks
Salt
2–3 green chillies
2 tablespoons olive oil
2 teaspoons turmeric
2 tablespoons coriander or parsley, chopped

1. Boil the potatoes in salted water until slightly under done and then drain.
2. Deseed and finely chop the chillies. Heat the olive oil in a large frying pan on a medium heat and stir in the chillies and turmeric.
3. Add the drained potatoes and fry until golden brown and tender. Serve hot or cold sprinkled with chopped coriander or parsley.

Oven-baked Potatoes with Mushrooms and Thyme

SERVES 4

This simple dish is so good and it is easy to make.

455g floury potatoes (e.g. King Edward), peeled and chopped into large chunks
55g Pure
1 egg yolk
Salt and pepper
½ nutmeg, grated
1 onion, finely chopped and fried
1 tablespoon parsley, chopped
1 tablespoon chives, chopped
Gluten-free plain flour
455g mushrooms
1 tablespoon olive oil
2 cloves garlic, chopped
1 teaspoon thyme, chopped
1 tablespoon dry sherry

1. Put your oven on at 200°C and brush a baking sheet with olive oil.
2. Cook the potatoes over a low heat and mash. Add the Pure, egg yolk, salt, pepper and nutmeg and beat well. Fold in the fried onion, parsley and chives.
3. Sprinkle your work surface with a little gluten-free flour. Divide the mash into 8 and shape into 10cm cakes. Bake in the oven for 15 minutes. Turn over and cook for another 15 minutes.
4. Cut the mushrooms into chunky slices and fry gently in the oil. Add the garlic, thyme, salt and pepper and fry for 2 minutes. Then add the sherry and cook for another 2 minutes. Serve the mushrooms heaped on top of the potato cakes.

SERVES 4–6

Potato Boulangére

This simple recipe can also be made with other root vegetables, such as parsnips or turnips. Just thinly slice and mix in with the layers of potatoes. Thinly sliced leeks are also very good as an addition.

55g Pure
1kg Desiree potatoes, peeled and thinly sliced
Salt and pepper
1 medium white onion, peeled and thinly sliced
15g fresh rosemary, bruised and chopped
2 cloves garlic, finely chopped
300ml vegetable stock
150ml soya milk
¼ nutmeg, grated

1. Put your oven on at 180°C. Wipe some of the Pure around the serving dish and then layer up potatoes, salt and pepper, onion, Pure, rosemary and garlic.
2. Combine the soya milk and stock and pour over. Dot some Pure over the top and sprinkle with nutmeg.
3. Cover with foil and cook for 1 hour. Remove the foil and continue cooking until the potatoes are tender.

Spicy Potatoes

SERVES 5–6

2 tablespoons groundnut oil
1 medium white onion, peeled and chopped
2 cloves garlic, finely chopped
2 teaspoons ground cumin
2 teaspoons ground coriander
½ teaspoon turmeric
¼ teaspoon cayenne
680g potatoes, peeled and cut into 2cm chunks
1 teaspoon salt
100g frozen peas, defrosted
1 teaspoon garam masala
4 tablespoons coriander, chopped

1. Warm the oil in a deep frying pan on a medium heat and add the onion. Cover and cook for 5 minutes.
2. Add the garlic, cumin, ground coriander, turmeric and cayenne and cook for 2 minutes.
3. Add the potatoes and stir to coat with the onion and spices.
4. Add the salt and 150ml of water, bring to the boil and then cook gently until just tender (10–15 minutes). They may need a stir half way through to prevent sticking but all of the water should be absorbed. Add the peas in the last few minutes of cooking.
5. Stir in the garam masala and garnish with chopped coriander. Serve hot or cold.

CHAPTER 6

A Perfection of Puddings and Cakes

Puddings are usually associated with lashings of cream and butter so can be out of the question for those who cannot tolerate dairy products. Many of these recipes contain mango or apricots, in place of cream, because they lend stability to the puds and the taste is just great. You don't feel at all deprived!

At a dinner party recently, our hostess served the most delicious soya ice cream, which is available from Waitrose. For somebody like me, who hasn't been able to have ice cream for years and years, it was nectar! I do recommend it highly, served with some of the following desserts. Fantastic!

Using gluten-free flour in some of these cakes and pastries can make them a little drier or crumblier than if you used other flours. Just add a pinch of a product called xanthan gum to the flour the pastry will be much easier to handle and the cakes not so crumbly. It is available in good supermarkets and can be found in the 'free from' section. Flour packets do recommend the amount of xanthan to add, but I found that this recommended quantity spoilt the taste, so just add a pinch.

Almond and Apricot Tart

SERVES 8–10

Pastry
125g Pure
225g gluten-free plain flour
50g icing sugar
½ egg, beaten
1–2 tablespoons soya milk

Filling
270g caster sugar
250g Pure
4 eggs
250g ground almonds
450g apricots, stoned and halved

1. First make the pastry. In a mixing bowl, combine the flour and sugar and then rub in the Pure. Bring together with the egg and a tablespoon or 2 of soya milk. Place in the refrigerator to chill for an hour and then line out a 30cm greased flan dish with the pastry. Chill again for about ½ hour.
2. Meanwhile, whizz the sugar and Pure in your food processor until light and fluffy, and then gradually add the eggs.
3. Put your oven on at 160°C. Mix in the ground almonds and heap this frangipani mixture into the flan case. Place the apricots, cut side up, in the mixture and dust with a little caster sugar.
4. Bake for about 1–1¼ hours or until firm.

MAKES 12

Apple and Cinnamon Buns

110g Pure
110g golden caster sugar
Pinch of xanthan gum
175g gluten-free plain flour
2 large eggs
1 teaspoon bicarbonate of soda
2 teaspoons cream of tartar
1 teaspoon ground cinnamon
50g ground almonds
175g apple, peeled and chopped
50g apple, peeled and diced

We have a cookery writer in our local magazine called Mrs Simkins, and this is one of her delicious cake recipes from her book *Tea with Mrs Simkins*, which I have adapted to become 'free from'.

1. Turn the oven on at 160°C and grease a 12-cup muffin tin or line one with muffin papers.
2. Whizz the Pure and sugar together in your food processor until light and creamy.
3. Add the xanthan gum to the flour and sieve over half. Blend slightly and add the eggs. Sieve the rest of the flour, bicarbonate, cream of tartar and cinnamon over the mixture and whizz briefly.
4. Add the almonds and whizz again.
5. Add the chopped apple and whizz until smooth and glossy. Fold in the remaining apple and divide the mixture into the bun cases.
6. Bake for about 20 minutes or until a skewer comes out clean.

Apple and Ginger Simnel Cake

SERVES 11

This cake is a delicious variation on the traditional simnel cake, which contains dried fruit and lemon. I have also made it without the marzipan balls but with Christmas decorations and it was very well received!

200g Pure
300g muscovado sugar
3 large eggs, 1 beaten
25g fresh ginger root, grated
Pinch of xanthan gum
200g gluten-free self-raising flour
1 cooking apple, peeled, cored and grated
200g crystallised stem ginger, finely chopped
250g white marzipan
A little apricot jam

1. Put your oven on at 170°C and line a loose-bottomed 20cm cake tin with Bakewell paper.
2. Melt the Pure and stir in the sugar. Cool slightly, beat in 2 eggs and the ginger root.
3. Stir the xanthan gum into the flour. Add the apple and the crystallised ginger and mix gently into the cooled sugar mixture. Put the mixture in the tin and bake for 1–1¼ hours or until a skewer comes out with just a few crumbs on it.
4. Heat the grill and roll 200g of marzipan into a 20cm circle. Make the remaining marzipan into 11 little balls.
5. Melt some apricot jam and brush over the top of the cake and place the circle of marzipan on top. Brush with the beaten egg. Place the balls around the top of the cake, brush again with the egg.
6. Place the cake underneath the grill until it reaches a golden brown. Decorate, when cool, as appropriate for the celebration.

SERVES 8

Apple and Maple Pandowdy

175g gluten-free plain flour
140g Pure
2 tablespoons caster sugar
Pinch of salt
Pinch of xanthan gum
1.5kg Bramley apples
70g light brown muscovado sugar
150ml maple syrup
Icing sugar

The taste of maple syrup is just so good I had to include this dish, even if it is really a glorified apple tart!

1. Put the flour and 125g of the Pure in a bowl and rub together until it forms breadcrumbs.
2. Add the caster sugar and salt and then add 1 tablespoon of cold water and a pinch of xanthan gum and bring together to form a ball. If it is too dry, add a little more water.
3. Knead lightly, wrap in cling film and chill for 15 minutes. Put the oven on at 180°C.
4. Peel, core and slice the apples. Put in a large bowl and sprinkle over the muscovado sugar. Toss the apple slices in the sugar and put into a baking dish. Pour over the maple syrup and dot over the remaining Pure.
5. Roll out the pastry and cut into squares. Arrange the squares on top of the apple so that they overlap in a higgledy-piggledy fashion. Cook for 1 hour until the apple is cooked and the top is golden. Dust with icing sugar before serving.

Apple Flapjack

MAKES 12

1 medium cooking apple
30g sultanas
140g light brown soft sugar
170g Pure
170g rolled oats
55g gluten-free wholemeal flour

These delicious flapjacks are only suitable if you have a wheat intolerance as opposed to a gluten allergy. However, they are so delicious, I thought that I would include them.

1. Peel, core and grate the apple and put into a saucepan with the sultanas and 30g of the sugar. Bring to the boil and simmer for 5 minutes until the apple thickens slightly.
2. Melt the Pure in another saucepan and stir in the oats, flour and the rest of the sugar.
3. Turn your oven on to 180°C. Spread half the oaty mixture in a 20cm square, lined tin and press down with the back of a spoon. Spread over the apple mixture and top with the rest of the oaty mixture.
4. Bake for 30–40 minutes. Leave to cool and cut into squares.

SERVES 5–6

Apricot and Papaya Fool

There is no added sugar in this recipe, which is good for some special diets.

140g ready-to-eat dried apricots, chopped
30g dried papaya, chopped
425ml sweetened soya milk
1 tablespoon lime juice
2 tablespoons rapeseed or flax oil
Strawberries or kiwi fruit to decorate
100g flaked almonds, toasted

1. Soak the apricots and papaya in the soya overnight. Liquidise and add the lime juice. Then add the oil and liquidise again.
2. Put into individual dishes, garnish with the sharp fruit and sprinkle over the almonds. Easy!

Apricot Compote

SERVES 8

The fruity flavours are really brought out by the star anise and vanilla in this dish.

500g dried apricots
2 tablespoons honey
2 star anise
2 whole cloves
1 vanilla pod
Grated zest of 1 orange
250ml fresh orange juice plus 250 ml of water

1. Put all the ingredients in a thick-bottomed saucepan, bring to the boil and then gently simmer for about 15 minutes.
2. Leave to chill and then remove the anise and vanilla pod. For a more summery effect, fold in raspberries or strawberries. Delicious!

SERVES 8

Apricot, Peach and Blackberry Crumble

600g apricots, stoned and quartered
3 peaches, stoned and sliced
400g blackberries
Grated zest of ½ lemon
Juice of 1 lemon
150g caster sugar
150g gluten-free plain flour
125g ground almonds
175g Pure
30g flaked almonds

The fruit for this recipe does need to be really ripe, but if it is not cook it slightly in advance.

1. Put your oven on at 180°C and put the fruit, lemon zest and juice into an ovenproof dish and stir in 40g of the sugar.
2. Make the crumble by mixing together the flour, ground almonds and remaining sugar. Rub in the Pure until it resembles breadcrumbs.
3. Put the crumble on top of the fruit, scatter with the flaked almonds and bake for 40 minutes or until the fruit is soft.
4. If the crumble is already golden at this stage but the fruit is still hard, cover with foil and continue cooking to soften the fruit.

Baked Apple and Almond Pudding

SERVES 8

This pudding is very easy to make and is a real British classic.

900g apples, peeled and sliced
210g soft brown sugar
220g Pure
210g golden caster sugar
4 large eggs
220g ground almonds
30g flaked almonds

1. Grease a 20 x 4.5cm pie dish and put your oven on at 180°C.
2. Put the apples in a saucepan with the brown sugar and 2 tablespoons of water. Simmer until soft and put into the pie dish.
3. Cream the Pure and the caster sugar until really pale and fluffy. Add the eggs slowly, beating all the time. Fold in the ground almonds.
4. Spread over the apples and sprinkle the flaked almonds on top. Bake for exactly 1 hour.

12 BARS

Blackberry and Almond Slice

100g Pure
200g plain flour
Pinch of xanthan gum
50g icing sugar
½ egg, beaten
150g bramble jelly or raspberry jam
125g butter
125g soft brown sugar
2 eggs, beaten
1 teaspoon vanilla extract
200g ground almonds
350g blackberries or raspberries or mixed
50g flaked almonds

This summer, I picked loads of blackberries from the hedgerows and used them for these slices.

1. To make the pastry, rub the Pure into the plain flour until it resembles fine breadcrumbs. Fold in the xanthan gum and icing sugar. Put ½ a beaten egg in the centre of the mix and bring together to form a soft dough. Chill well in the freezer for 1 hour or in the refrigerator for about 2 hours.
2. Put your oven on at 180°C. Line a 21 x 30cm tin with Bakewell paper. Then roll the pastry and line the tin. If you find it difficult to handle the pastry, roll it into 2 pieces, put them into the tin and gently finger the join to give a smooth base.
3. Prick with a fork and bake for 15 minutes. Then spread the jam over the pastry.
4. Beat the butter and sugar until light and fluffy. Beat in the eggs gradually.
5. Add the vanilla and fold in the ground almonds. Spread this over the jam in the tin, and then press the fruit down into it.
6. Cook for 10 minutes. Then sprinkle with the flaked almonds and cook for 10–15 minutes more or until firm to touch.

Carrot Cake Pudding

SERVES 8

250ml sunflower oil
225g golden caster sugar
3 large eggs
250g carrots, grated
225g gluten-free self-raising flour
Handful of walnuts, chopped

This delicious pudding is wonderful served with a gluten and dairy-free ice cream with a little ginger syrup spooned over it. Alternatively, heat a little Seville and ginger marmalade with some water and spoon this over the pudding.

1. Put the oven on at 180°C. In your food processor, whizz the oil and caster sugar until thick.
2. Add the eggs one by one, still whizzing.
3. Add the carrots and gently fold in the flour and the nuts. Put into an 18 x 28 x 2½cm tin.
4. Bake at for about 45 minutes or until a skewer comes out clean. Serve as above. This pudding freezes very well.

MAKES 16

Chocolate and Courgette Brownies

175g courgettes, peeled and cut into short lengths
110g Pure
175g dark brown sugar
2 teaspoons cream of tartar
1 teaspoon bicarbonate of soda
50g good quality cocoa powder
Pinch of xanthan gum
250g gluten-free plain flour
3 eggs, lightly beaten
1 teaspoon vanilla extract

Our allotment went into overdrive on the courgette production, so I was very pleased to find this delicious recipe for these wonderfully moist little cakes! This is another delicious Mrs Simkins' recipe.

1. Grease and line a 20cm square brownie tin. Put your oven on at 160°C.
2. In your food processor, with the ordinary blade, whizz the courgettes into strands.
3. Add the Pure and the sugar and whizz to combine.
4. Add the cream of tartar, bicarbonate, cocoa powder and xanthan gum to the flour and sieve half of it over the mixture.
5. Add the eggs and vanilla and sieve over the rest of the flour combination. Whizz until smooth and well mixed.
6. Pour this mixture into the cake tin, easing into the corners. Bake for about 30 minutes. Test by inserting a skewer – it should just show a very slight trace of the mixture. Mark into squares and leave to cool.

Dorset Apple Cake

SERVES 8

A delicious traditional cake to eat hot or cold. I used to sell hundreds of these at farmers' markets.

Pinch of xanthan gum
280g gluten-free self-raising flour
140g Pure
120g light brown sugar
1½ teaspoons mixed spice
85g sultanas
455g cooking apples, peeled, cored and chopped into small chunks
1 large egg
140ml soya milk
Demerara sugar to sprinkle

1. Put your oven on at 160°C. Add the xanthan gum to the flour. Rub together with the Pure, sugar and spice to form fine breadcrumbs.
2. Add the sultanas and apples and fold together.
3. Mix together the egg and soya, add to the mixture and combine.
4. Put into a lined 900g loaf tin and sprinkle with Demerara sugar.
5. Bake for about 45 minutes or until a skewer inserted into the cake comes out clean. If you can resist eating the whole thing immediately, keep in the refrigerator as the apple will tend to go mouldy after a few days, or slice it up and keep in the freezer.

SERVES 10

Chocolate, Pear and Hazelnut Truffle Tart

300g blanched hazelnuts
200g gluten-free flour
1 tablespoon cocoa powder
Pinch of xanthan gum
50g icing sugar
Pinch of salt
125g Pure
1 egg yolk

Filling
150g 75% dark chocolate, roughly broken up
75g plain gluten-free flour
150g light brown sugar
75g Pure
2 egg yolks, beaten
½ teaspoon vanilla extract
3 ripe pears, peeled, cored and sliced

This is rich and delicious!

1. Put the oven on at 180°C and toast 275g of the hazelnuts until golden. Then whizz in a food processor until ground, but still textured. Remove from the processor.

2. Add the flour, xanthan gum, cocoa powder, icing sugar and a pinch of salt to 50g of the toasted nuts and whizz to combine.

3. Add the Pure and mix to form breadcrumbs. Then add the egg yolk and pulse to a dough.

4. Remove from the processor and roll into a 14 x 7cm sausage. Chill for 30 minutes.

5. Slice the chilled dough about 5mm thick and lay the slices in a 25cm tart tin, slightly overlapping them as you go. Press down and bring the dough up the sides of the tin. Prick all over with a fork and chill for another 30 minutes.

6. Line with Bakewell paper, fill with baking beans and cook in your preheated oven for 10 minutes. Remove the beans and paper and cook for another 10 minutes.

7. To make the filling, whizz the remaining 225g of toasted nuts with the broken up chocolate until finely chopped.
8. Add the flour and sugar, and briefly whizz. Then add the Pure, egg yolks and vanilla and whizz to make a smooth paste.
9. Put the filling evenly into the chocolate case and push the pears in slightly to make a pattern. Press the 25g of untoasted hazelnuts over the top.
10. Bake for 20–25 minutes until *just* firm to touch. Scrumptious!

SERVES 8

Chocolate Roll

This is my most requested pudding of all time!

Filling
225g couverture chocolate
2 large eggs, separated

Base
6 large eggs, separated
140g caster sugar
55g cocoa powder
Icing sugar to dust

1. First make the filling. Melt the chocolate and 2 tablespoons of water in a bowl over hot water, but do not overheat or allow the bowl to touch the water. Whisk in the 2 egg yolks and switch off the heat.
2. Whisk the 2 egg whites until they are really stiff. Pour over the chocolate mixture and fold into the whites, very gently, until fully amalgamated.
3. Cover with film wrap and refrigerate for at least 4 hours.
4. Turn the oven on to 180°C. Line a 34 x 24cm Swiss roll tin with Bakewell paper.
5. Now make the base. Whisk the 6 egg yolks and sugar until it is only just starting to thicken. Do not over whisk.
6. Add the cocoa and whisk until smooth but once again do not over whisk. The mixture should be soft.
7. In a separate bowl, whisk the 6 egg whites to a soft peak but not over dry and fold into the chocolate mixture, gently, until the whites are fully absorbed.

8. Spread this mixture in the tin and bake for 15–20 minutes until the roulade is springy to touch and firm but not dry.
9. Dust a piece of greaseproof paper with icing sugar. Remove the base from the oven, leave to cool and then turn over onto the greaseproof paper.
10. When the roulade is completely cold, spread the chocolate mousse over right up to the sides.
11. Roll up from the widest side, tucking the roulade in and under very firmly to start with so that it forms a nice roll. This is important otherwise you will end up with a chocolate sandwich shape! Use the greaseproof paper to help you roll. Keep wrapped up in the refrigerator until it is set and then roll it onto your serving dish.
12. For a special occasion you can make this into a black forest version by draining off a tin of black pitted cherries, adding some brandy and allowing them to soak for at least 4 hours. Drain these off and sprinkle over the mousse before rolling up. Put the brandy residue in a glass and imbibe!

SERVES 6

Coconut and Mango Fool

200g block of creamed coconut
2 medium tins mangoes in syrup
4 cardamom pods
2 tablespoons lime juice
Strawberries or sliced lime to garnish

Make sure that the juice content in the purée is sufficient, otherwise the pud will be a bit stodgy.

1. Melt the coconut very gently in a little water.
2. Liquidise the mango with a little syrup to make a purée which just holds its shape – not too thick!
3. Take the cardamom seeds out of their pods and grind in a pestle and mortar. Add to the warm, sticky coconut.
4. Add the mango and lime juice and stir well. Add more lime juice if you like it a little sharper.
5. Garnish with strawberries or lime slices.

Vanilla Baked Pears with Chocolate Sauce

SERVES 4

This pear dish is not so expensive to make as the recipe using marsala, but it is equally as good.

110g caster sugar
Rind of ½ lemon, pared in a long strip
1 vanilla pod, split lengthways
4 pears, peeled but still with their stalks intact
100g flaked almonds

Chocolate sauce
165g plain chocolate, broken up
55g Pure

1. Pour the sugar into a saucepan, add the lemon rind, vanilla pod and 300ml of water. Dissolve the sugar over a moderate heat.
2. Put the pears into the liquid and simmer on a low heat, covered, until just cooked.
3. Put the pears into a serving dish and then reduce the syrup by boiling for about 5 minutes. Pour some juice over the pears and leave to cool.
4. Toast the flaked almonds on a baking sheet in a pre-heated oven at 180°C for about 10 minutes or until nicely golden.
5. To make the chocolate sauce, put the chocolate, Pure and 4 tablespoons of water into a bowl and heat through over a pan of simmering water. Make sure that the bottom of the bowl does not touch the water. Whisk the sauce together until it is smooth and shiny and then pour over the pears.
6. Sprinkle over the toasted almonds before serving.

SERVES 8

Cranberry and Orange Tart

Pastry
Pinch of xanthan gum
125g gluten-free flour
70g Pure
35g icing sugar
1 egg yolk

Filling
150g dried cranberries
Juice of 1 orange and ½ lemon
115g Pure
115g caster sugar
2 large eggs
30g gluten-free flour
115g ground almonds
Grated zest of orange
6 tablespoons fine marmalade
40g hazelnuts, toasted and chopped
Icing sugar to dust

I love this pudding with its contrasting content of sharpness and richness. It can be cut into squares and served as a cake if you prefer. It will also freeze well.

1. Add the xanthan gum to the flour and put it with the Pure and sugar in a food processor. Whizz until it forms fine, golden breadcrumbs.
2. Add the egg yolk, with 1 tablespoon of water if it is little too dry. Leave to chill in the freezer for about an hour or in the refrigerator for longer if you have the time.
3. Put the cranberries in a saucepan with half of the fruit juices and simmer for 10 minutes. Remove from the heat and leave the cranberries to plump up.
4. Put your oven on at 180°C. Line a 20cm greased flan dish with the pastry and cover with Bakewell paper and baking beans. Bake blind for 10 minutes. Remove the paper and beans and bake for another 5 minutes and then put to one side. Reduce the oven temperature to 160°C.

5. Beat the Pure and sugar until really light and fluffy and gradually add the eggs, beating all the time.

6. Then stir in the flour, almonds, orange zest and the rest of the fruit juices.

7. Spread the marmalade over the pastry, spoon on the cranberries and then spread the almond mixture over.

8. Scatter over the nuts and bake for 30–40 minutes until firm and golden. Dust with icing sugar when cooled.

MAKES 8

Flapjacks

120g Pure
120g soft brown sugar
85g golden syrup
170g quinoa flakes

Such a traditional cake, which can be made with quinoa flakes so that it is suitable for coeliacs. You can also add a handful of raisins and/or chopped hazelnuts for added interest.

1. Put your oven on at 170°C. Melt the Pure, sugar and golden syrup over a gentle heat and stir until they are combined into a sauce. Fold in the quinoa.
2. Line a 20cm square tin or tray with non-stick paper. Put the flapjack mixture in the tray and bake for 20–30 minutes until light golden. Do not overcook or it will be rock hard!
3. Remove from the oven and, after about 10 minutes, cut into required sizes with a sharp knife.

Florentines

MAKES 40 COCKTAIL SIZE

These are the crispiest Florentines that I have ever found. We used to make hundreds for wedding receptions.

- 170g Pure
- 335g caster sugar
- 65g runny honey
- 250g glacé cherries, chopped
- 335g flaked almonds, chopped
- 85g mixed peel
- 85g sultanas
- 335g couverture chocolate (or the best cooking chocolate that you can afford)

1. Over a gentle heat melt together the Pure, caster sugar and honey in a saucepan, stirring to a sauce-like consistency.
2. Add the cherries, almonds, peel and sultanas to the honey mixture. Stir well and then put the oven on at 180°C.
3. Put a little of the mixture in well greased mince pie tins and bake for 10–15 minutes until golden. You can use greaseproof cake papers here to prevent them sticking. If overcooked they will taste bitter, and if undercooked they will be soggy, so a good deep golden colour is best.
4. Leave to cool until just warm and then run a knife around each tin and put the Florentines on a rack to finish cooling (or press them out of the cake papers).
5. Melt the chocolate in a bowl over a pan of hot water, without allowing the bowl to touch the water. With a dessertspoon, spread a little on the base of each Florentine. Leave to set upside down on a sheet of Bakewell paper.
6. These are delicious served with Vanilla Baked Apricots.

SERVES 8

Lemon and Poppy Seed Cake

140g caster sugar
140g Pure
2 large eggs, beaten
Pinch of xanthan gum
140g gluten-free self-raising flour
30g black poppy seeds
Grated zest of 1 lemon
180ml soya milk
2 tablespoons icing sugar
Juice of 1 lemon

While on holiday in Oxfordshire we visited Daylesford Organic shop and tasted their poppy seed cake, which was divine. So I now make a 'free from' version, which is also very good, I think!

1. Line a 455g loaf tin with Bakewell paper and put your oven on at 180°C.
2. Beat the sugar and Pure until really pale and then gradually add the beaten eggs.
3. Add the xanthan gum to the flour and sift in. Add the poppy seeds and the lemon zest.
4. Add enough soya milk to make a soft, dropping consistency.
5. Put in the mixture in the tin and cook for about 45 minutes or until a skewer inserted comes out clean.
6. Combine the icing sugar and lemon juice and warm in a saucepan. Stab the cake with a skewer and pour over the sugar/lemon mixture. Leave to cool.

Mango Rice Pudding

SERVES 8

This is incredibly Asian in flavour and delicious – not at all like our English rice pudding from school days!

3 ripe mangoes
1 litre soya milk
150g basmati rice
120g soft brown sugar
50g raisins
50g slivered almonds (flaked are also fine)
1 teaspoon rose water or elderflower cordial
Large pinch of saffron
1 teaspoon ground cardamom
Pistachio slivers to garnish

1. Peel the mangoes. Slice the flesh into a liquidiser and purée.
2. Bring the milk to the boil and then reduce to a simmer and pour in the rice. Stir off and on for 25 minutes until the rice is soft.
3. Turn off the heat and add the sugar and stir until dissolved. When tepid stir in the mango purée and add the remaining ingredients.
4. Chill and sprinkle over the pistachio slivers.

SERVES 8 AS A PUD OR 16 SLICES

Paradise Slice or Pudding

Pastry
200g gluten-free plain flour
Pinch of xanthan gum
50g ground almonds
25g golden caster sugar
125g Pure
1 large egg

Topping
200g Seville orange marmalade
225g golden caster sugar
75g ground almonds
100g dessicated coconut
200g Pure
2 large eggs
125g ground rice flour
Grated zest of 1 orange
160g raisins

1. Put your oven on at 180°C. Rub together the flour, xanthan gum, almonds, sugar and Pure to form golden crumbs. Add the egg and bring together, adding a tablespoon of water if too dry. Chill the pastry in the refrigerator.
2. Line a 20cm flan tin or Swiss roll tin with Bakewell paper. Then line with the pastry and bake blind for 15 minutes.
3. Remove from the oven and spread with the marmalade. Lower the oven temperature to 150°C.
4. Whizz the sugar, almonds and coconut in the food processor and then add the Pure, eggs and rice flour and whizz again.
5. Stir in the orange zest and raisins and spread over the pastry. Bake for 40 minutes until golden brown. Cut when cool.

Paradise Chocolate Slices

MAKES 12

Fantastic slices for coconut and chocolate lovers.

300g chocolate
100g Pure
200g caster sugar
2 medium eggs
200g desiccated coconut
100g sultanas
100g glacé cherries

1. Turn on your oven to 140°C and line a 20 x 30cm Swiss roll tin with non-stick parchment.
2. Melt the chocolate in a bowl over simmering water and then run it out over the parchment and leave to set.
3. Cream the Pure and caster sugar and slowly add the eggs. Fold in the coconut, sultanas and cherries and then spread over the chocolate.
4. Cook for 25 minutes until pale golden brown. Cool and cut to your choice of size. They are quite rich!

SERVES 8

Parsnip Cake

2 large eggs
125ml sunflower or rapeseed oil
250g caster sugar
Zest of 1 lemon
1 teaspoon vanilla essence
350g parsnips, grated (250g grated weight)
Pinch of xanthan gum
375g gluten-free self-raising flour
½ teaspoon ground cinnamon
½ teaspoon salt
60g walnut pieces, chopped

I saw parsnip cake on the menu in a coffee shop in Suffolk and had to try it out of interest. It was delicious. And after trying out a few recipes, I found that this was the best one. Spread it with Pure before eating for sheer indulgence!

1. Put your oven on at 160°C. Whisk the eggs, oil, sugar, lemon zest and vanilla until really thick. Stir in the parsnips.
2. Add the xanthan gum to the flour and sift with the cinnamon and salt into a bowl. Make a well in the centre. Pour in the parsnip mixture and bring together with a large spoon. Fold in the nuts.
3. Put into a 455g loaf tin or 20cm cake tin and bake for 60–80 minutes or until a skewer inserted comes out clean. Dredge with icing sugar when cold.

Pear and Apple Crumble

SERVES 8

You can use rhubarb in place of pears for this traditional pudding.

2kg mixed Bramley apples and cooking pears (or rhubarb)
Grated zest and juice of 1 orange
¼ teaspoon nutmeg, freshly grated
1 teaspoon ground cinnamon
50–75g granulated sugar

Crumble
125g gluten-free plain flour
150g hazelnuts, toasted and chopped
25g rolled oats (or quinoa flakes)
½ teaspoon ground cinnamon
75g light brown soft sugar
50g Demerara sugar
125g Pure

1. Put your oven on at 160°C. Peel and slice the fruit and put into a shallow ovenproof dish.
2. Grate over the orange peel and pour over the orange juice. Sprinkle with the nutmeg, cinnamon and granulated sugar.
3. Mix all the crumble ingredients to a breadcrumb consistency and put over the fruit. Bake for about 40 minutes until golden and the fruit is soft.

SERVES 8

Pear and Gingerbread Upside-down Pudding

170g Pure
120g light brown soft sugar
3 cooking pears
80ml (80g) molasses
85ml (85g) honey
2 large eggs
240g ginger marmalade
40g crystallised ginger
200g gluten-free self-raising flour
Pinch of xanthan gum
1 teaspoon mixed spice
½ teaspoon ground nutmeg
½ teaspoon ground cinnamon
½ teaspoon allspice
½ teaspoon mace

Ginger is such a wonderful ingredient to use in puddings and, combined with the pears, well I think it is the perfect mix.

1. Grease a 23cm round and 5cm deep tin and line with Bakewell paper. Put your oven on at 160°C.
2. Melt the Pure in a saucepan over a medium heat and pour half into a mixing bowl.
3. Whisk half the sugar with the rest of the Pure, in the pan, until blended. Spread over the base of the tin.
4. Peel and core the pears, cut into thin slices and arrange in the tin so that they overlap. Dice and set aside any remaining pear.
5. In your mixer or processor, beat the molasses and honey with the remaining sugar and Pure. Add the eggs one at a time, still beating, and then add the marmalade.
6. Finely chop the ginger and add.

7. Sieve the flour, xanthan gum and spices and fold into the mixture, with the remaining pears. Spread over the arranged pears and cook for about 1¼ hours or until firm in the middle.
8. Cool for a few minutes and then invert over a large plate. Remove the Bakewell paper and serve warm or cold.

SERVES 6

Pear Chocolate Betty

1kg pears
30g Pure
125g soft white gluten-free breadcrumbs
75g light brown soft sugar
100g dark cooking chocolate, chopped
75g Pure, melted
3 tablespoons golden syrup

When there is a glut of pears in the autumn, this pudding is just the thing to make and enjoy.

1. Put your oven on at 190°C. Cut the pears into large chunks and put in a saucepan with 30g of Pure. Add 2 tablespoons of water and soften over a medium heat. Shake occasionally and when soft but not soggy, tip into a shallow baking dish.
2. Mix the breadcrumbs, sugar and chocolate together and scatter over the pears.
3. Add the melted Pure to the golden syrup and heat until blended. Pour over the crumbs to cover all areas. Bake for about 35 minutes.

Pears in Marsala Wine

SERVES 8

The Florentines from earlier in this chapter are rather good to eat with these pears.

- 8 firm cooking pears
- ½ litre marsala wine
- 55g golden caster sugar
- 2 whole cinnamon sticks
- 1 vanilla pod
- 1 rounded dessertspoon arrowroot
- 50g walnuts, roughly chopped

1. Put your oven on at 120°C. Peel the pears and cut a little off the bases so that they stand firmly.
2. Put the pears on their sides in a deep casserole dish. Pour over the marsala, sprinkle with sugar and add the cinnamon and vanilla.
3. Poach gently for 1–1½ hours, turning the pears over half way through. They should be tender but firm. Cool in the liquid.
4. Drain off the marsala and put a little in a bowl. Heat the rest in a saucepan. Blend the cold marsala with the arrowroot and add to the saucepan, stirring all the time. Chill and pour over the pears. Sprinkle with the walnuts.

SERVES 6

Pommes Lorraine

125g raisins
225ml orange juice
1kg eating apples, cored and peeled
125g light brown sugar
Grated zest and juice of 1 lemon
150g gluten-free wholemeal breadcrumbs
80g Pure

Simple, quick and very, very good with vanilla soya ice cream.

1. Put the raisins and orange juice in a small pan. Bring to the boil and simmer for 5 minutes. Leave to plump up.
2. Grease a 25 x 20 x 5cm baking dish with some Pure and put your oven on at 180°C. Thinly slice half of the apples and arrange in the dish. Sprinkle with half of the sugar, raisins and liquid and lemon zest and juice.
3. Scatter over half of the crumbs and dot with half of the Pure. Repeat this process.
4. Cook until the top is golden brown and the apples just tender.

The Ultimate Free-from Fruit Cake

SERVES APPROX. 8

You would not think that this recipe would work – but it does!

450g mixed dried fruit
Juice of 1 fresh orange
225g cooking dates (not sugar rolled)
175g gluten-free self-raising flour, sifted
Pinch of xanthan gum
1 teaspoon mixed spice
Grated rind of 1 lemon
Grated rind of 1 large orange
40g ground almonds
A few flaked almonds

1. Soak the mixed dried fruit in the orange juice over night.
2. Line a 900g loaf tin with baking parchment and put the oven on at 160°C.
3. Put the dates in a saucepan with 275ml of water. Cook very gently until the dates are soft.
4. Mash up the dates and add the soaked dried fruit, sifted flour and xanthan gum, spice, grated rind and ground almonds. Fold together and spoon into the tin. Level the top and sprinkle with the flaked almonds.
5. Bake for about 1½ hours.

SERVES 6–8

Vanilla Baked Apricots

20 apricots, halved and stoned
1 vanilla pod
400ml white wine
160g caster sugar

Anything involving vanilla attracts my taste buds and this dish most certainly does just that!

1. Put on your oven at 180°C. Lay the apricots, skin-side up, in overlapping circles in a serving/baking dish.
2. Split the vanilla pod and scrape out the seeds. Tuck the pod under the fruit and add the seeds to the white wine. Pour the wine over the fruit and sprinkle over the sugar.
3. Bake for 20 minutes or until the sugar is slightly caramelised. Serve warm for full flavour or cold with ginger snaps or florentines.

CHAPTER 7

Odds and Ends

This chapter contains a small collection of additional foods to make some of the other dishes in this book even more delicious. They are all very easy to make, cost so much less than the manufactured versions, do not contain anything you would rather not put into your body and taste much nicer, I think!

SERVES 4–6

Aubergine Sauce for Pasta

3 tablespoons olive oil
1 large red onion, chopped
3 cloves garlic, chopped
1 teaspoon ground cumin
1 medium aubergine, chopped
3 ripe tomatoes, peeled and chopped
Seasoning
Good handful of basil leaves

1. Heat the oil in a heavy pan, add the onion and fry over a low heat until softened.
2. Add the garlic and cumin and cook for another minute.
3. Stir in the aubergine and cook gently until soft and beginning to brown.
4. Add the tomatoes to the sauce. Season and simmer until collapsed.
5. Fold in the chopped basil leaves, reserving some to sprinkle over when the sauce is poured over pasta.

Beetroot Relish

MAKES 1.4kg

455g cooking apples, peeled, halved and cored
455g raw beetroot, trimmed and peeled
335g onion, finely chopped
150g sultanas
1 teaspoon salt
1 tablespoon ginger root, finely chopped
2 large cloves garlic, finely chopped
1 teaspoon paprika
1 teaspoon turmeric
1 cinnamon stick
225g soft brown sugar
400ml red wine vinegar
Salt and pepper

1. Grate the apple and the beetroot into a large pan and then add the remaining ingredients.
2. Bring to the boil, stirring, and then reduce the heat and cover the pan.
3. Cook, stirring occasionally, until the relish thickens.

SERVES 6

Fresh Tomato Sauce

1.35kg ripe tomatoes
1 tablespoon olive oil
3 small onions, finely chopped
3 cloves garlic, finely chopped
3 teaspoons tomato purée
3 dessertspoons basil, chopped
Salt and pepper

1. Peel the tomatoes by first pouring over boiling water and leaving for a few minutes. Then chop them quite small.
2. Heat the olive oil, add the onion and garlic and cook until the onion is soft.
3. Add the tomatoes, tomato purée, basil, salt and pepper.
4. Simmer gently for 15 minutes, covered. Uncover the pan and simmer for another 10 minutes to reduce slightly.
5. Give a very short whizz in the food processor, taste and adjust the seasoning as necessary.

Ginger Onion Marmalade

SERVES 4

350g onions
2 tablespoons olive oil
3 rosemary sprigs
225ml dry white wine
3 tablespoons white wine vinegar
1 tablespoon red wine vinegar
2 tablespoons soft dark sugar
2 rounded dessertspoons ginger, freshly grated
Salt and pepper

1. Slice the onion into rings. Heat the oil in a saucepan over a gentle heat and add the onion with the rosemary. Toss around until golden and tinged brown at the edges.
2. Pour in the wine and vinegar. Add the sugar, ginger, salt and pepper and simmer over a low heat for 1¼ hours. The liquid should almost have disappeared after this time. And that is it. Easy and delicious!

SERVES 4

Lentil and Walnut Pâté

110g red lentils
½ onion, chopped
1 clove garlic, chopped
250ml vegetable stock
30g walnuts, chopped
2 teaspoons cider vinegar
2 teaspoons Marmite
1 teaspoon soya milk
1 dessertspoon dates, chopped
1 tablespoon rapeseed oil
2 heaped teaspoons thyme, chopped
Seasoning

Use this pâté as a spread on toast, rice cakes or as a dip with crisps.

1. Place the lentils in a saucepan and cover with water. Bring to the boil. Drain and return to the pan with the onion, garlic and vegetable stock. Bring to the boil and then simmer for 20 minutes.
2. Drain and stir in the other ingredients.
3. Put in your liquidiser and process to your preferred texture. I think that it is best with a little texture. Season.

Mini Pancakes

MAKES 20 COCKTAIL SIZE

These are excellent as a starter as well as a cocktail nibbler, with your own choice of toppings.

- 4 tablespoons wild rice
- 2 tablespoons basmati rice
- 55g gluten-free flour
- ¼ teaspoon salt
- 1 egg
- ½ teaspoon ground coriander
- 4 tablespoons soya milk
- 2 tablespoons spring onion, finely chopped
- 1 tablespoon sunflower oil
- Seasoning

1. Put the wild rice in a saucepan with 8 tablespoons of water. Simmer with the lid on over a low heat or until the rice is nutty but tender. Drain and cool.
2. Put the basmati in a separate saucepan. Add 2 tablespoons of water, a pinch of salt and cook covered over a low heat until the water has been absorbed and the rice is tender. Drain and cool.
3. Mix the flour, salt, egg, coriander and soya milk to a smooth batter and stir in the onion and rice. Season.
4. Brush the frying pan with oil and drop heaped teaspoons of the mixture into the pan. Cook for 2–3 minutes on each side.
5. You can keep them in the refrigerator for a day or two, or in the freezer. Refresh them in a hot oven before topping and serving.

Toppings

Both these toppings can be used for the pancakes on page 151.

Salsa

1 small avocado, finely chopped
½ medium red onion, finely chopped
Juice of 1 lime
1 tablespoon olive oil
Salt
Tabasco sauce
2 spring onions, finely chopped

Combine all ingredients and leave to marinate for an hour or so.

Lime Mayonnaise

4 tablespoons mayonnaise
Lime juice to taste
Coriander

Combine the ingredients.

OR anything else you fancy!

Mushroom Pâté

SERVES 4

55g Pure
1 small onion, finely chopped
1 teaspoon coriander seeds, crushed
350g mushrooms, sliced
Salt and pepper
25g creamed coconut
1 tablespoon dark soy sauce
50g gluten-free, preferably brown breadcrumbs

It is always so difficult to buy pâtés that do not include butter or gluten. This recipe is so quick, tasty and easy to do, that you won't need to pick your way around shop shelves for pâté ever again!

1. Melt the Pure in a saucepan over a gentle heat and add the onion. Cook until soft and transparent.
2. Add the crushed coriander seeds and fry for 1 minute over a gentle heat. Add the mushrooms and cook until soft.
3. Season and stir in the coconut, soy sauce and breadcrumbs.
4. Put in the food processor and blend until smooth. Check the seasoning and adjust to your taste.

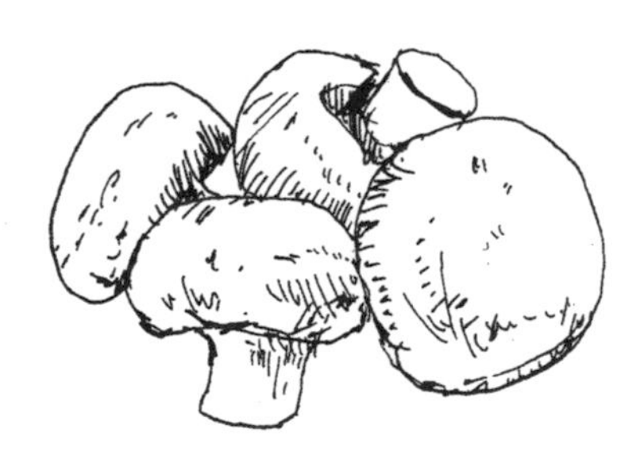

Olive, Almond and Walnut Spread

95g black olives, stoned and finely chopped
95g ground almonds
4 tablespoons unsalted capers, washed, drained and chopped
Salt and pepper
30g walnuts, finely chopped

This is a very piquant spread and delicious on rice cakes, bread rolls, etc. It wil keep for approximately 6 days in the refrigerator.

Mix all of the ingredients except for the walnuts together into a paste in your liquidiser or food processor, adding a little water to make a spreadable consistency. Fold in the walnuts.

Variation
Use sundried tomatoes in place of the olives and add roughly chopped basil.

Pear and Apple Chutney

6 pears, cored and cubed
3 cooking apples, cored and cubed
1 large onion, finely chopped
10 cherry tomatoes, quartered
400g brown sugar
150g sultanas
75g dried apricots, chopped
500ml cider vinegar
250ml dry cider or dry white wine
1 tablespoon grain mustard
2 cloves garlic, finely chopped
½ teaspoon cinnamon
½ teaspoon ground cinnamon
1 teaspoon dried sage
1 teaspoon dried oregano

1. Put all of the ingredients into a large, stainless steel saucepan. Cook gently, stirring, until the sugar has dissolved.
2. Continue to simmer for about 1½ hours until the mixture has thickened.

Pesto Sauce

50g fresh basil leaves
1 large clove garlic, crushed
1 tablespoon pine kernels
6 tablespoons olive oil
Seasoning

Keep this sauce in a jar in your refrigerator to use on salads, pastas, baked potatoes, roasted vegetables to give a real zing to things!

Put all of the ingredients into your liquidiser and whizz until smooth. Season well.

Red Onion Marmalade

MAKES 2 JARS OF APPROX. 455g

2 oranges, unpeeled but chopped and deseeded
1 lemon, chopped and deseeded
225g red onion, chopped
250ml vegetable stock
225g dark brown sugar
4 teaspoons arrowroot
140ml apple pectin

1. Place the oranges, lemon, onion and vegetable stock in a saucepan and bring to the boil. Simmer for 30–40 minutes until the orange and lemon rind is tender.
2. Add the sugar and boil for 4 minutes, stirring occasionally.
3. Add the arrowroot and stir continuously as the liquid thickens.
4. Remove from the heat and stir in the pectin. Cool a little and store in closed jars.

Rhubarb Chutney

10 large tomatoes, quartered
1kg rhubarb, sliced
2 large, white onions, chopped
225g sultanas
225g Demerara sugar
600ml malt vinegar

1. Prepare your chutney pots. Wash the pots, rinse and drain. Then put them into your oven on a tray at 150°C for about 10 minutes. This sterilises the pots and prevents them breaking when the hot chutney is poured in.
2. Heat the tomatoes in a large saucepan over a gentle heat until they collapse.
3. Add the rhubarb, onion and sultanas and slowly bring to the boil, stirring continuously.
4. Add the sugar and simmer to melt, still stirring. Pour over the vinegar and keep stirring until the chutney thickens.
5. Cool slightly. Then add the chutney to the prepared and still hot pots and seal.

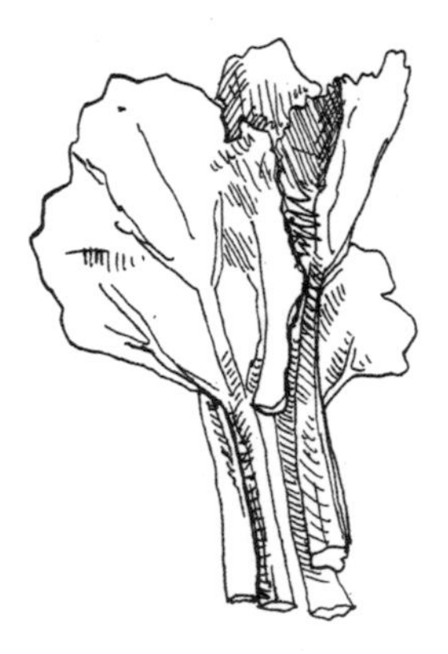

Runner Bean Chutney

This recipe was an entry in our village cookbook, published to raise funds for the church, and it is really tasty. The chutney is ready to eat after a couple of months but is particularly good after about 6 months.

900g runner beans, strung and chopped (prepared weight)
680g onions, chopped
850ml malt vinegar
2 tablespoons gluten-free flour
1 teaspoon turmeric
1 teaspoon mustard powder (check for gluten content)
A few sultanas or raisins depending on how sweet you like your chutney
790g Demerara sugar
1 teaspoon salt

1. Cook the prepared beans in boiling salted water until just tender.
2. Boil the onions in 275ml of the vinegar until tender.
3. Mix the flour, turmeric and mustard powder to a paste, with a little of the remaining vinegar.
4. Add the rest of the vinegar, the beans and sultanas or raisins to the onion mix and cook together over a medium heat for about 10 minutes, stirring occasionally.
5. Add the sugar, the turmeric paste and the salt, stir well and bring to the boil. Simmer without the lid on for a further 10 minutes. Leave to one side for 10 minutes.
6. Meanwhile, prepare your chutney pots. Wash the pots, rinse and drain. Then put them into your oven on a tray at 150°C for about 10 minutes. This sterilises the pots and prevents them breaking when the hot chutney is poured in.
7. Add the chutney to the hot pots and seal.

Salad Dressings

Herb and Citrus

- 1 teaspoon sesame oil
- 2 tablespoons rapeseed oil
- 2 tablespoons olive oil
- 2 tablespoons lemon juice
- Salt and freshly milled black pepper
- 2 small handfuls of mixed herbs, freshly chopped (e.g. mint, parsley and chives)
- 1 teaspoon caster sugar
- Grated rind of ½ small orange
- Juice of ¼ small orange
- 2 teaspoons wholegrain mustard

Put the oils and lemon juice in a screw-top jar and shake well. Season and add the remaining ingredients and shake very well. Leave to stand and shake again before dressing your salad.

Lemon, Soy and Honey

- 2 tablespoons lemon juice
- 1½ tablespoons wheat-free soy sauce
- 1 tablespoon clear honey
- 2 tablespoons rapeseed oil
- 2 teaspoons walnut oil
- 3 pinches of chilli powder

Just put all the ingredients together and whisk or shake well.

Sweet and Sour Onion and Tomato Relish

SERVES APPROX. 4

This relish is delicious with millet burgers or other vegetable burgers. It is quite hot and spicy so adapt the quantity of chillies depending upon your palate.

- 2 tablespoons corn oil
- 2 teaspoons brown sugar
- 2 cloves garlic, halved
- 1 onion, chopped
- 1 level teaspoon salt
- ¼ teaspoon dried red chilli, crushed
- 1 fresh green chilli, deseeded and sliced
- 3 tablespoons malt vinegar
- 2 large tomatoes, deseeded and sliced
- 1 green pepper, deseeded and sliced
- 1 tablespoon fresh coriander, roughly chopped
- 1 dessertspoon tomato purée

1. Heat the oil in a small saucepan over a gentle heat, sprinkle with the brown sugar and fry lightly. Add the garlic and onion and fry for 2 minutes.
2. Add the salt and chillies and stir around. Then lower the heat.
3. Add the vinegar, tomatoes, green pepper and coriander. Cook for 5 minutes. Stir in the tomato purée.

Index